Right to Education

A New Right to a New Education

By

A. Reis Monteiro

Right to Education: A New Right to a New Education

By A. Reis Monteiro

This book first published 2024

Ethics International Press Ltd, UK

British Library Cataloguing in Publication Data

A catalogue record for this book is available from the British Library

Print Book ISBN: 978-1-80441-512-2

eBook ISBN: 978-1-80441-513-9

Table of Contents

Chapter 2
New Education

Chapter 3
Answering some questions

Introduction
By what right do we educate?

Education is a complex theoretical-practical field of research because the educational phenomenon is multiform, multidimensional, multidisciplinary.

The educational phenomenon raises the primordial anthropological question of human educability, but the central question of pedagogic thought has been that of the purpose of education, that is, the question of the values and principles that should inspire and guide it. However, the most radical one, nowadays, concerns its legitimacy, that is the question of the source, sense and control of the power the education exerts, through the contents and forms of the communication it accomplishes. It should be considered its *meta-question* or the question of questions. It is such a radical question that it has been generally *unthinkable*. For the traditional pedagogical mindset, educating is so *natural* that the question of the legitimacy of education is dissolved in this assumption: (As) education is necessary, (whatever) education is legitimate. It is fallacious reasoning because it does not distinguish between necessity and legitimacy.

To problematise the legitimacy of education is to question the *pedagogic* as the traditional signifier of validity claims concerning education:

- What is pedagogic?
- Is what is useful? But whom for?
- Is what is efficient? But what for?
- Is what parents, teachers, Ministries of Education, say and order? But with what legitimacy?
- By what right human beings do what they do over human beings in the name of education?

Boldly put: *By what right do we educate?*

In the age of human rights – and especially of the rights of the child – the most legitimate response to the *meta-question of the legitimacy of education* should be researched in the *right to education*.

In children's education, different interests are involved and sometimes confronted, all claiming entitlement to the 'right to education'. However, education and *human right* to education may be different things. That is why the first United Nations Special Rapporteur on the Right to Education (Katarina Tomaševski, 1998-2004) wrote in her Preliminary Report (E/CN.4/1999/49)[1]:

> 8. … A simple but crucial question – what does full realization of the right to education entail? – will thus orientate the work of the Special Rapporteur.
>
> …
>
> 13. … The Special Rapporteur therefore attaches a great deal of importance to emphasizing differences between *education* and the *right to education* [original emphasis] so as to create a background for advocating changes within education aimed at conformity with the human rights requirements.

The right to education being about 'right' and 'education', the Special Rapporteur wrote in another Report (E/CN.4/2001/52)[2]:

> 69. … The orientation and contents of education can only be studied in close collaboration between educationalists and human rights lawyers, and the Special Rapporteur is very much looking forward to this collaborative effort.

This book aims at briefly and clearly highlighting the "differences between *education* and the *right to education*". Its contents are as follows:

- Chapter 1 presents an overview of human rights and the rights of the child – highlighting their ethical revolutionary significance – as a general framework necessary to know and understand the specificity of the right to education. Thereafter, the respective international profile is outlined, and its singularity and priority are emphasised, especially the consubstantiality with human dignity. It is concluded that the emergence and development of the right to education is a new chapter of the History of Education and has given rise to an International Education Law.

- Chapter 2 proposes a conceptualisation for the operationalisation of the normative content of the right to education, that is, for drawing its juridical-political-pedagogical implications. It is encapsulated in the concept of Rightful Education, which is systematised in Principles of Ethics of the Right to Education from which stem Educational Rights. It is concluded that a Rightful Education requires a Right to Education Pedagogy and Policy, as well as the recognition of new Sciences of Education.

- Chapter 3 offers short answers – in the light of the preceding chapters – to questions on issues more familiar to public opinion and others. They are examples of the juridical-political-pedagogical outcomes of a *human right approach* of education.

The Conclusion highlights the revolutionary significance of the right to education. The Appendices add the main universal normative framework of the right to education, as well as extracts from the Education Agenda of the International Community, and a classical question is revisited.

This is an *essential* edition, summarising, updating and upgrading the main results of the author's research and theorising on the right to education as a human right. Without prejudice to rigour and depth, backed up by a documentary counterpoint of endnotes, it aims at a wide audience with interest in human rights, children's rights and, in particular, the right to education, including mothers and fathers more concerned with the education of their sons and daughters. For this reason, it does not contain authors' quotations and bibliography (except for three poets, but poetry is not and has not bibliography). Only international instruments and documents are quoted, as well as international and national Case Law. Also, the use of abbreviations/ acronyms unfamiliar to lay readers is generally avoided.

This book can serve as a brief and accessible Introduction to International Education Law. The subject matter is much more developed in two other publications, each with its own academic apparatus: *Revolution of the Right to Education* (Brill|Sense, 2021) and *Introdução ao Direito da Educação – Internacional, Europeu e Português* (Introduction to Education Law – International, European and Portuguese, Lisbon International Press, 2023).

I'm grateful once again to Emily Griffith at Deakin University Law School, Australia, for the careful revision of the linguistic accuracy of the manuscript.

Chapter 1
New Right

1.1 Human rights

1.1.1 Origins and concept

- **Origins**

Human rights have no date or place of birth. They have emerged slowly, like a dawn, from the night of times, in East and West, in South and North, expressing sentiments and aspirations as timeless and cross-cultural as human suffering and the ideal of Justice. This is illustrated by the unique and beautiful anthology *Le droit d'être un homme* (Birthright of Man), published by UNESCO (United Nations Educational, Scientific and Cultural Organisation) in the context of the 20th anniversary of the Universal Declaration of Human Rights. Think of the Code of Hammurabi (Babylon, 18th century BC), the Ten Commandments (13th century BC), the Charter of Cyrus (Persia, 4th century BC), the Magna Carta or The Great Charter of Liberties of England (1215), the Bill of Rights (England, 1689), the 18th century American and French Revolutions and Bills of Rights.

We may distinguish three main stages in the modern and contemporary history of human rights:

- Philosophical elaboration of the old 'natural rights' idea (17th – 18th centuries)
- Bills of Rights and their constitutionalisation (18th – 20th centuries)
- Internationalisation of human rights (after World War II)

The universalisation of the principle of respect for human rights began with the Charter of the United Nations (UN), drawn up by the San Francisco Conference (US), whose proceedings took place from 25 April to 26 June 1945, the day on which the Charter was signed by 50 States (plus one a little later). It entered into force on 24 October of the same year, now celebrated as United Nations Day. The Nazi Third Reich had capitulated on 8 May, after 5 years and 8 months of an unprecedented world war. According to the UN Charter[3], one of its objectives is "promoting and encouraging respect for human rights and for fundamental freedoms for all without distinction as to race, sex, language, or religion" (Article 1.3).

The first far-reaching legal instrument devoted to human rights by an Intergovernmental Organisation (IGO) was the American Declaration of the Rights and Duties of Man, adopted on 2 May 1948 by the IX American International Conference, in Bogota (Colombia), that had adopted the Charter of the Organisation of American States (OAS) on 30 April.

On 10 December 1948, the UN General Assembly, meeting in Paris, proclaimed the Universal Declaration of Human Rights, for 48 votes to none against, with 8 abstentions. The Declaration was drafted by the Commission on Human Rights established by the Economic and Social Council (ECOSOC), first as 'Nuclear Commission', on 16 February 1946. The full Commission, composed of 18 elected members, held its first session in New York from 27 January to 10 February 1947.

The history of human rights juridification, that is, of their moral claims becoming Law, is frequently presented as a 'generations' succession, reflecting the trilogy of the French Revolution: *Liberté, Égalité, Fraternité* (Liberty, Equality, Fraternity).

- *First generation* ('liberty rights' or 'negative rights': *freedoms from…*): they are the civil and political rights proclaimed by the 18th century Bills of Rights, progressively incorporated into constitutional texts, becoming a cornerstone of liberal democracies.

- *Second generation* ('equality rights' or 'positive rights': *rights to*...): they are the economic, social and cultural rights which emerged during the 19th century and developed in the 20th century, claimed principally by the socialist ideologies as conditions of enjoyment of the liberties.

- *Third generation* ('solidarity rights' or 'collective rights': *new rights*): they are such rights as the right to peace, the right to sustainable development, the right to healthy environment, the right to be different, which took the floor since the 1960s as demands of new realities and threats.

There is talk of a *fourth generation* of rights, which are mainly those related to new information and communication technologies, such as "the right to the protection of personal data concerning him or her" (right to informational self-determination) recognised in the Charter of Fundamental Rights of the European Union (Article 8)[4], the right of access to Internet (see 2.3.8), the right to be forgotten...

The 'generations' distinction is controversial, however, for several reasons. The classic freedoms began to be constitutionally recognised before economic, social and cultural rights, but these ones began to internationalise first, with the establishment of the International Labour Organisation (ILO) as part of the Versailles Peace Treaty (Part XIII) that, following the Paris Peace Conference, formalised the end of World War I, in 1919, and included the Covenant of the League of Nations. In addition, a right may be both 'first generation' and 'second generation', as is the case of the right of trade union association. Some rights have a transversal content, especially the right to life and the right to education. Moreover, the distinction may suggest a misleading hierarchisation of rights.

The largest international conferences on human rights to date have been:

- International Conference on Human Rights, in Tehran (Iran), from 22 April to 13 May 1968, with the participation of 84 States. It adopted the *Tehran Proclamation* and 29 Resolutions (apart from other 18 ones especially addressed to the UN bodies).

- World Conference on Human Rights, in Vienna (Austria), from 14 to 25 June 1993. It gathered about 7000 participants, among them representatives of more than 170 States and about 800 Non-governmental Organisations (NGOs). It adopted the Declaration and Programme of Action of Vienna which has become the human rights reference of the UN system.

- **Concept**

Every human community and society needs rules, written or not, to make living together according to common values possible, and to meet common needs. This is the meaning of the Latin saying, *Ubi societas, ibi jus* (Where there is society, there is Law).

Positive, written Law is a coercive normative order, that is, whose violations are sanctioned. It has expanded as a network framing international, national and individual lives, becoming the most powerful driver of Civilisation. In the contemporary world, there is no other alternative for the peaceful coexistence of cultures, peoples and the human diversity.

There are Law (objective) and rights (subjective) – a terminological distinction specific to the English language. Law is the body of written normativity forming a legal order. Rights are prerogatives attributed to individuals by Law. The rights of a person constitute her legal personality.

A right is, therefore, a normative position that confers on someone a freedom or faculty, to which obligations correspond (passive or active) on the part of others, individuals or entities. The recognition and protection of rights by Law distinguishes them from purely moral rights.

Human rights are a higher category of rights. According to the most elementary definition, they are rights recognised to every human being just because (s)he is a member of the human species. Human rights are therefore universal and qualified as "equal and inalienable".

- *Equal* because they are held by every human being, without any discrimination, in all circumstances, everywhere.

- *Inalienable* because they are never lost, that is, they cannot forcibly be taken away (by expropriation) or voluntarily given up (by transaction).

'Imprescriptible' is another term used in 18th century Bills of Rights, but it has practically fallen into disuse. The idea of imprescriptibility (inextinguishability) is subsumed in that of inalienability (which needs to be nuanced, however).

Human right is an open concept. Higher Courts sometimes refer to the living nature of human rights instruments, which must be interpreted teleologically, that is, taking into account their spirit and purpose. Scientific-technological progress and social changes, in addition to influence how human rights are exercised, create the need to recognise new rights.

In 1986, the UN General Assembly adopted a Resolution on "Setting international standards in the field of human rights" (A/RES/41/120)[5]. In it: "*Recognising* the value of continuing efforts to identify specific areas where further international action is required to develop the existing international legal framework in the field of human rights", the General Assembly proposed "guidelines in developing international instruments in the field of human rights". *Inter alia*: "Be of fundamental character and derive from the inherent dignity and worth of the human person".

The UN Charter (1945) and the 1948 Universal Declaration are at the origin of a new branch of International Law: International Human Rights Law.

1.1.2 International Human Rights Law

- **Specificity**

Classical International Law, predominant until World War II, was dominated by the principles of sovereignty and consent of States – its exclusive actors – which accepted obligations only of a contractual, reciprocal nature.

State sovereignty remains the basis of the international political order, as provided for by the UN Charter (Article 2.7, inherited from Article 15.8 of the Covenant of the League of Nations, and echoing in UNESCO's Constitution Article I.3), but it is eroding, increasingly shifting to institutions building up the International Community.

Human rights are not a matter "essentially within the domestic jurisdiction" (Article 2.7 of the Charter)[6]. The Charter mentions them seven times. According to its Article 56: "All Members pledge themselves to take joint and separate action in co-operation with the Organisation for the achievement of the purposes set forth in Article 55", one of which is promoting "universal respect for, and observance of, human rights and fundamental freedoms for all without distinction as to race, sex, language, or religion"[7]. The Universal Declaration of Human Rights has been proclaimed by a Resolution of the UN General Assembly.

International Human Rights Law is not subject to the principle of reciprocity. In it, States have no self-interest, but a common interest: the protection of the human rights of all persons under their jurisdiction, which is an obligation *erga omnes* (towards all, towards the whole International Community), as the Human Rights Committee pointed out at the beginning of its General Comment 31 (CCPR/C/21/Rev.1/ Add. 13, 2004)[8]:

> 2. While Article 2 is couched in terms of the obligations of States Parties towards individuals as the right-holders under the Covenant, every State Party has a legal interest in the performance by every other State Party of its obligations. This follows from the fact that the 'rules concerning the basic rights of the human person' are *erga omnes* obligations. [...] Furthermore, the contractual dimension of the treaty involves any State Party to a treaty being obligated to every other State Party to comply with its undertakings under the treaty. [...] Accordingly, the Committee commends to States Parties the view that violations of Covenant rights by any State Party deserve their attention. To draw attention to possible breaches of Covenant obligations by other States Parties and to call on them to comply with their Covenant obligations should, far from being regarded as an unfriendly act, be considered as a reflection of legitimate community interest.

International Human Rights Law thus has both a vertical valence (the principal one, concerning the obligations of States Parties towards all persons under their jurisdiction) and a horizontal valence (concerning obligations between States Parties).

International Human Rights Law may be defined narrowly or broadly:

- Narrowly defined, its object includes the legal dimensions of human rights: their sources, normative content, mechanisms of protection, jurisprudence, doctrine[9].

- Broadly defined, it is an interdisciplinary field of research to which legal and other disciplines contribute, whose scope should include the study of the human dignity principle, of the history of human rights and the repercussions of their recognition (and violations) in the life of individuals, peoples and the future of the human species.

- **Normative sources**

Prior to World War II, custom was viewed as the principal source of International Law, binding on all States. Customary International Law consists mainly of General Principles of Law, common to most legal systems as a kind of universal juridical conscience, as was the ancient

Jus Gentium (Law of Nations), formed of rules dictated by *recta ratio* (right reason).

After World War II, Customary International Law was largely codified, notably in the Vienna Convention on the Law of Treaties (1969), and Treaty Law has developed as the main source of International Law. According to the canonical Article 38.1 of the Statute of the International Court of Justice, annexed to the UN Charter[10], the Court applies "international conventions", "international customs", "the general principles of law", as well as "judicial decisions and the teachings of the most highly qualified publicists of the various nations, as subsidiary means for the determination of rules of law".

The *Corpus Juris* (Body of Law) of International Human Rights Law comprises hundreds of legal instruments – universal and regional, conventional and declaratory, with general, specific or categorical content.

- Universal are legal instruments adopted within the United Nations institutional framework or under its auspices.

- Regional are legal instruments covering a continent or region, such as those adopted by the Council of Europe or the Organisation of American States.

- Conventional are legal instruments formally binding States Parties, such as treaties and other equivalent instruments.

- Declaratory are legal instruments not formally binding, with varying denominations, adopted by Intergovernmental Organisations, such as the UN General Assembly.

- General are legal instruments that include all categories of human rights or some of them.

- Specific are legal instruments concerning a sole right (the right to education, for example).

- Categorical are legal instruments aiming to reinforce the protection of a more vulnerable category of persons (children, for example).

The most general universal normative framework of International Human Rights Law is the International Bill of Human Rights, which is not a legal instrument. It designates a set of three instruments adopted by the United Nations: Universal Declaration of Human Rights (1948), International Covenant on Civil and Political Rights (1966) and International Covenant on Economic, Social and Cultural Rights (1966).

Besides the two 1966 International Covenants, there are more seven treaties adopted within the United Nations framework, forming the *core human rights treaties*, namely:

- International Convention on the Elimination of All Forms of Racial Discrimination (1965)

- Convention on the Elimination of All Forms of Discrimination against Women (1979)

- Convention against Torture and Other Cruel, Inhuman or Degrading Treatment or Punishment (1984)

- Convention on the Rights of the Child (1989)

- International Convention on the Protection of the Rights of All Migrant Workers and Members of their Families (1990)

- Convention on the Rights of Persons with Disabilities (2006)

- International Convention for the Protection of All Persons from Enforced Disappearances (2006)

These nine treaties, which are complemented by Protocols (short treaties), form a system of protection against the most serious violations of human rights and to reinforce the protection of more vulnerable categories of human beings. Their application is supervised by

Committees. All UN Member States have ratified at least one of them, and 80% have ratified four or more. The International Covenant on Civil and Political Rights was so far ratified by 173 States (and signed by 6 more) and the International Covenant on Economic, Social and Cultural Rights was so far ratified by 171 States (and signed by 4 more)[11].

At the regional level – European, American, African and in other regions – the main legal instruments on human rights are the following:

- European Convention for the Protection of Human Rights and Fundamental Freedoms (European Convention on Human Rights)

  (Council of Europe, 1950, now with 16 Protocols, some of them incorporated into the Convention)

- European Social Charter

  (Council of Europe, 1961, with Protocols, revised in 1996)

- American Declaration of the Rights and Duties of Man

  (Organisation of American States, 1948)

- American Convention on Human Rights (Pact of San José de Costa Rica)

  (Organisation of American States, 1969, now with 2 Protocols)

- Additional Protocol to the American Convention on Human Rights in the Area of Economic, Social and Cultural Rights (Protocol of San Salvador)

  (Organisation of American States, 1988)

- Social Charter of the Americas

  (Organisation of American States, 2012)

- African Charter on Human and Peoples' Rights (Banjul Charter)
  (Organisation of African Unity (OAU, replaced by the African Union in 2002), 1981, now with 2 Protocols)

On the European continent, there are two more instruments:

- Charter of Fundamental Rights of the European Union, adopted by the European Union (EU) at the European Council meeting held in Nice (France) on 7 December 2000, which applies only to the implementation of the European Union Law by its institutions and Member States. It became binding on 1 December 2009 with the entry into force of the Treaty of Lisbon Amending the Treaty on European Union and the Treaty Establishing the European Community, which had been signed at Lisbon on 13 December 2007[12].

- Commonwealth of Independent States Convention on Human Rights and Fundamental Freedoms (Minsk, Belarus, 1995)[13]

The League of Arab States, established in 1945, sitting in Cairo, adopted in 1994 an Arab Charter on Human Rights, revised in 2004 and entered into force in 2008. The League is partly overlapped by the larger Organisation of Islamic Co-operation (OIC), founded in 1969 as Organisation of the Islamic Conference, sitting in Saudi-Arabia, that adopted in 1990 the Cairo Declaration on Human Rights in Islam that subjects human rights interpretation and application to Islamic Law.

In the Asia-Pacific region, the Association of Southeast Asian Nations (ASEAN) adopted a Human Rights Declaration (2012) and other texts.

There are human rights provisions in other branches of International Law, including International Labour Law, International Environmental Law, International Health Law, International Refugee Law, International Humanitarian Law and International Criminal Law.

Let us better explain the distinction between conventional and declaratory instruments.

- Conventional instruments are those creating international legally binding obligations. This is the so-called 'Hard Law' (*lex lata*: Law enacted) that goes by a variety of denominations: Treaty, Convention, Covenant, Protocol, Charter, etc. (38 names were identified). A treaty is self-executing when it is domestically immediately effective, without need of implementing legislation to be enforceable, or non-self-executing, when it requires ancillary legislation in order to be judicially implemented.

- Declaratory instruments are those not legally binding, creating rather moral and political obligations. This is the so-called 'Soft Law' (*lex ferenda*: Law in the making) that also goes under a variety of denominations: Declarations, Recommendations, Resolutions, Principles, Directives, Codes of Conduct, Frameworks for Action, Commentaries, Opinions, etc. mainly adopted within the framework of the United Nations and other Intergovernmental Organisations. Despite its name, Soft Law is not of minor importance. It frequently includes norms already having customary or conventional legal force, contributes to the emergence of new rights and paves the way for the adoption of instruments of a conventional nature.

The most striking example of the influence of a Soft Law instrument is the Universal Declaration of Human Rights – the mother of International Human Rights Law. There is virtually no instrument of International Human Rights Law not invoking it, notably those adopted by the UN General Assembly. In the opinion of many scholars, the principles and rights proclaimed by the Universal Declaration (or most of them) have become Customary International Law.

- **Terminology**

In the UN Charter (Preamble) and in the International Bill of Human Rights we find the expressions "fundamental rights", "fundamental human rights", "fundamental rights and freedoms", "human rights and fundamental freedoms", "human rights and freedoms", "rights and freedoms", "rights or freedoms". Other terms are 'civil rights' and *libertés publiques* (public liberties/freedoms). No significant conceptual distinction can be drawn between "rights" and "freedoms". Both terms appear together sometimes. For example: "Everyone shall have the right to freedom of thought, conscience and religion."

A distinction exists between *human rights* and *citizens' rights*. Although they are generally closely tied, they should be distinguished. In a Rule of Law, citizens' rights include universal human rights and other rights held only by nationals (especially political rights).

Although the Anglophone expression *human rights* has become the most common, the classic French expression *droits de l'homme* (Rights of Man) continues to circulate in the French-speaking world.

In constitutional texts, the most used expression is "fundamental/basic rights", consecrated by the 1919 German Constitution of Weimar, whose Part II, echoing the 1849 Frankfurt Constitution, was titled *Grundrechte und Grundpflichten der Deutschen* (Fundamental/basic rights and duties of Germans).

1.1.3 Structure and normative content of human rights

Human rights are the answer of International Community to this question: What do human beings need to live free "from fear and want", as reads the Preamble to the Universal Declaration of Human Rights?

The International Bill of Human Rights lists some 40 rights[14] which, according to the denominations of the 1966 International Covenants, fall into five categories (by alphabetical order): civil, cultural, economic, political, social. They aim at protecting the weakest against the strongest – especially States – as well as guaranteeing to everyone a minimum of autonomy and self-determination, for living a decent and meaningful life, i.e. by providing every human being with food, shelter, health care, etc., as well as conditions of participation in cultural, social and political life, thus generating feelings of self-worth and self-esteem.

Each right has a structure and normative content that answer the following main questions:

- Who holds the right (entitlement: right-holders)?
- To what is it a right (object)

- o Who has the corresponding obligations (exigibility: duty-bearers)?

Holders of human rights are, by definition, "everyone", "every human being", "all persons", except when a legal instrument addresses a more vulnerable category of persons (women, for example).

Some rights have a collective dimension, when their exercise involves interaction with other people, as are typically the right of assembly and the right of association; and there are rights collectively recognised to minority communities (indigenous peoples, for example). In any case, collective rights should never be exercised to the detriment of individual rights.

Each right proclaims and protects a fundamental human value and lays down the interdictions and/or the actions/provisions it requires. It is its object. The normative specificity of each right is essentially determined by it.

The exigibility of a human right refers to those to which the right is opposable, that is, who bear obligations and responsibilities towards its fulfilment.

All rights are necessary for the "common standard of achievement" proclaimed by the Universal Declaration of Human Rights (last paragraph of the Preamble). Their interdependence was proclaimed by the International Covenants of 1966, in their common Preamble, and solemnly reaffirmed by the two major international conferences on human rights (Tehran, 1968, and Vienna, 1993). It is a principle and leitmotif of the texts adopted by the UN General Assembly.

1.1.4 Obligations concerning human rights

According to the Vienna Convention on the Law of Treaties (1969)[15], an international obligation of States is the recognition of the primacy of International Law over the national legal order (Article 27).

States – the authors and direct addressees of International Law – are the first human rights duty-bearers. All UN Member States have human rights obligations under its Charter. In addition, they have obligations under the treaties they ratify (an act formally binding to their application) and other relevant international norms they approve. Therefore, as the Committee on the Rights of the Child said in the Report of its 22nd Session (1999) (CRC/C/90, para. 269)[16]: "After the adoption of an international treaty, implementation faces two initial challenges: the translation of the international legal obligations enshrined in the Convention into domestic legal obligations, and the translation of domestic laws into reality by means of their day-to-day implementation."

States' human rights obligations are generally typified in the following trilogy: to respect, to protect, to fulfil.

- *To respect*

  States, including entities acting on their behalf, have an obligation to refrain from interfering with the enjoyment of human rights, at the vertical level of their relationship with people under their jurisdiction.

- *To protect*

  States have the obligation to set up mechanisms to prevent and to remedy human rights violations by public authorities or individuals and other private actors.

- *To fulfil*

  States have an obligation to enable persons to really enjoy their rights, whatever their social, economic or other condition.

These obligations are then "both negative and positive in nature", as the Human Rights Committee said (CCPR/C/21/Rev.1/Add. 13, 2004, para. 6)[17].

States may have extraterritorial obligations too. They "are a missing link in the universal human rights protection system", following the Maastricht Principles on Extraterritorial Obligations of States in the Area of Economic, Social and Cultural Rights (2011)[18], because without them "human rights cannot assume their proper role as the legal bases for regulating globalization and ensuring universal protection of all people and groups". According to Principle 8:

> For the purposes of these Principles, extraterritorial obligations encompass:
>
> a) obligations relating to the acts and omissions of a State, within or beyond its territory, that have effects on the enjoyment of human rights outside of that State's territory; and
> b) obligations of a global character that are set out in the Charter of the United Nations and human rights instruments to take action, separately, and jointly through international cooperation, to realize human rights universally.

Extraterritorial obligations arise, for instance, in situations where a State holds temporary control over populations in other territories, in the case of occupation or with an international mandate. They include its actions or omissions related to international cooperation, and as member of international organisations, as well as regulation and supervision of the activities in other countries of international non-State actors based in its territory, such as transnational corporations.

The Human Rights Committee said (CCPR/C/21/Rev.1/Add. 13, 2004, para. 6)[19] that no restriction on any rights in the Covenant may "be applied or invoked in a manner that would impair the essence of a Covenant right". The same said the Committee on Economic, Social and Cultural Rights (E/1991/23)[20]:

> 10. ... the Committee is of the view that a minimum core obligation to ensure the satisfaction of, at the very least, minimum essential levels of each of the rights is incumbent upon every State Party. Thus, for example, a State party in which any significant number of individuals is deprived of essential foodstuffs, of essential primary health care, of basic

> shelter and housing, or of the most basic forms of education is, *prima facie,* failing to discharge its obligations under the Covenant. If the Covenant were to be read in such a way as not to establish such a minimum core obligation, it would be largely deprived of its *raison d'être.* [...] In order for a State Party to be able to attribute its failure to meet at least its minimum core obligations to a lack of available resources it must demonstrate that every effort has been made to use all resources that are at its disposition in an effort to satisfy, as a matter of priority, those minimum obligations.

Before, the Committee had said:

> 8. ... In this regard, the Committee reaffirms that the rights recognized in the Covenant are susceptible of realization within the context of a wide variety of economic and political systems, provided only that the interdependence and indivisibility of the two sets of human rights [the two Covenants], as affirmed *inter alia* in the preamble to the Covenant, is recognized and reflected in the system in question.

The notion of each human right minimum/substance/essence is also found in constitutional texts[21].

In the light of these two imperatives – minimum content and interdependence of human rights – the object of a human right may be described as a normative complex made up of three layers, so to speak, to which correspond so many levels of obligations on the part of States Parties, namely:

- *Minimum obligation/content*

  It defines the level of guarantee of a right below which it loses its essence/substance, becoming meaningless.

- *Full obligation/content*

  It concerns all the elements/entitlements of a human right scope, formally laid down in its provisions or implied by them.

- *Expanded obligation/content*

  It includes elements of other rights that influence and condition a human right fulfilment.

International Human Rights Law allows for three modalities of self-limitation of States' obligations:

- *reservations* (if they are permitted) and *declarations of interpretation,* expressed when signing or ratifying a treaty;
- *restrictions* (limitations), in exceptional circumstances;
- *derogations* (suspensions), under restricted conditions;

Very few rights are considered absolute and non-derogable, untouchables (the identification of which varies in the main treaties).

The Declaration and Program of Action of Vienna (1993)[22] begins by stating (Preamble) "that the promotion and protection of human rights is a matter of priority for the international community". Although the existence of a formal right to international co-operation is not consensual, it is mentioned in the UN Charter and in several human rights instruments. Seeking international assistance and co-operation may be an obligation. There is an international obligation to help when States do not have the capacity to meet their obligations due to lack of resources. In the event of an active, serious, massive and systematic violation of human rights, there is even an obligation to intervene, according to the "Responsibility to Protect" assumed by a United Nations Summit in 2005[23].

The promotion and protection of human rights is a general responsibility, as proclaimed by the long title of the Declaration on the Right and Responsibility of Individuals, Groups, and Organs of Society to Promote and Protect Universally Recognised Human Rights and Fundamental Freedoms (United Nations, 1998)[24]. A fundamental principle of International Criminal Law is the principle of personal criminal responsibility, regardless of status or orders received, which should never be amnestied or time-barred (see Convention on the Non-

Applicability of Statutory Limitations to War Crimes and Crimes against Humanity, 1968, and the Rome Statute of the International Criminal Court, 1998)[25].

The first responsibility of each and every one is, however, to himself/herself: to know, to claim and to exercise one's rights is a duty towards the personal dignity, the communities in which we live and the common humanity.

1.1.5 Protection and justiciability of human rights

- **Protection**

The Vienna Declaration and Programme of Action (1993)[26] has recalled: "Human rights and fundamental freedoms are the birthright of all human beings; their protection and promotion is the first responsibility of Governments." (I.1) As reads the Preamble of the Universal Declaration of Human Rights, "it is essential [...] that human rights should be protected by the rule of law". The Rule of Law, democratic and social, is the best shelter of the human dignity and rights[27].

The UN General Assembly adopted, in 1993, "Principles relating to the Status of National Institutions (The Paris Principles)" (A/RES/48/134)[28], whose names and mandates are variable: *Ombudsman* or *Ombudsperson*, the name of the first Swedish institution of its kind (established in 1809), *Defensor del Pueblo, Défenseur des Droits de l'Homme,* Human Rights Commission, etc.[29]

Nevertheless, this is the double paradox of human rights: they are born against the State, but need protection and provisions by State; however, if States should be their main guarantors, they are often their main violators. This is why there are international systems/regimes for the protection of human rights at the universal and regional levels.

The UN universal system is made up of twofold mechanisms: Charter-based and Treaty-based.

- The mechanisms based on the UN Charter have been set up by the Economic and Social Council, in particular the Human Rights Commission, established in 1946. In 2006, it was replaced with the Human Rights Council, whose great novelty is the Universal Periodic Review (UPR) of the human rights situation in every UN Member States, which takes place every four and a half years.

  The Council has maintained the so-called '1503 Procedure', established in 1970 so that the Commission could receive and inquire into complaints of "consistent patterns of gross and reliably attested violations of all human rights and all fundamental freedoms" [Resolution 1503 (XLVIII)]. The former Sub-Commission on the Promotion and Protection of Human Rights was replaced with an Advisory Committee, composed of 18 experts.

  There are also Special Procedures (*Procédures Spéciales*) set up by the Commission, which consist of mandates for the promotion of human rights, with various denominations: Special Rapporteurs, Independent Experts, Working Groups, as well as Special Representatives of the Secretary-General.

- The conventional mechanisms, known as Treaty Bodies or Treaty Monitoring Bodies, are non-permanent Committees established by the core human rights treaties, with the exception of the Committee on Economic, Social and Cultural Rights, which was established by the Economic and Social Council. Their main functions are as follows:

  - *Supervision*

    This function consists of examining the reports of the States Parties on the implementation of the treaties they have ratified, presented at regular intervals. The review ends with "Concluding Observations" or "Concluding Comments", which note the positive aspects and point to the negative ones of the human rights situation, followed by recommendations.

- *Interpretative*

  This function is exercised principally through "General Comments" or "General Recommendations", which are documents elaborating on a Committee's understanding of a specific right or on transversal questions of the respective treaty, with the purpose to help States Parties implement it. The Committees are the most authoritative interpreters of the treaties whose implementation they supervise.

- *Quasi-judicial*

  This function concerns "Communications" or petitions/ complaints about alleged human rights violations addressed to UN Committees. Their decisions are sometimes qualified as "quasi-jurisprudence" because, although they are not true tribunals, competent to take formally binding decisions, they have their main attributes (legal basis, independence and motivation of decisions).

The Human Rights Committee meets in New York, but the other ones meet in Geneva.

The members of the Committees and of the Special Procedures are independent human rights experts serving in their personal capacity and working *pro bono* (without monetary retribution), but the Human Rights Council is an intergovernmental and permanent body, subsidiary to the UN General Assembly, made up of 47 members elected by UN regional groups.

In 1993, following the Vienna Conference, a United Nations High Commissioner for Human Rights (UNHCHR) was established, sited in Geneva UN Headquarters, with a Delegation in New York and offices worldwide. In 1997, it absorbed the Centre for Human Rights (which had been created in 1982 to replace the Division of Human Rights created in 1946). It coordinates the UN activities in the human rights field, providing secretariat services to the bodies involved in their protection. The High Commissioner has the rank of Under-Secretary-General.

UNESCO, ILO, the World Health Organisation (WHO) and the Food and Agriculture Organisation (FAO) are UN "specialised agencies" for the protection of some human rights. The International Committee of the Red Cross, guardian of the International Humanitarian Law, plays a unique role in the protection of human rights in war scenarios.

At the regional level, there are the European, American and African systems, established in order to take into account geographical and cultural particularities.

- *The European system*, established by the Council of Europe (1949), is the oldest, most effective and exemplary one. Its basis is the European Convention on Human Rights (1950) that instituted the European Commission of Human Rights (Article 49 of the original text), created in 1954, and the European Court of Human Rights (created in 1959), sitting in Strasbourg (France), which have merged in a Permanent Court on 1 November 1998. A European Commissioner on Human Rights was established in 1999. Its mandate is principally concerned with information and education.

  There is also a European Committee of Social Rights to monitoring compliance with the European Social Charter (1961, revised in 1996). Its supervisory mechanism consists of a reporting system and the examination of collective complaints.

  Within the European Union, the founding treaties of the European Communities, in the 1950s, did not include human rights. It was the Court of Justice of the European Communities (now Court of Justice of the European Union) that laid down the foundations of a community legal system of protection of the fundamental rights, in its decision on the *Case Stauder* (1969). A European Union Agency for Fundamental Rights was established in 2007 as an advisory body.

There is still the Organisation for Security and Co-operation in Europe (OSCE, 1990), formerly Conference on Security and Co-operation in Europe (CSCE, 1975), headquartered in Vienna.

- *The American system,* established by the Organisation of American States (1948), whose headquarters are in Washington, D.C., is based on the American Declaration of the Rights and Duties of Man (1948) and in the American Convention on Human Rights (1969). Its organs are the Inter-American Commission of Human Rights (created in 1959), sitting in Washington, D.C., and the Inter-American Court of Human Rights (created in 1969) that sits in San José, Costa Rica.

- *The African system,* established by the Organisation of African Unity (1963, replaced with the African Union in 2002), is based on the African Charter on Human and Peoples' Rights (1981). There is an African Commission on Human and Peoples' Rights (created in 1987), sited in Banjul, Gambia, and an African Court on Human and Peoples' Rights, sitting in Arusha, Tanzania (created in 1998). In 2008, it merged with the Court of Justice of the African Union into an African Court of Justice and Human Rights (which has not yet taken office).

In the Asia-Pacific region, there is no similar system of human rights protection. However, two regional organisations have adopted instruments and set up some mechanisms for the protection of human rights: Association of Southeast Asian Nations (ASEAN, 1967), sitting in Jakarta (Indonesia), and South Asian Association for Regional Co-operation (SAARC, 1985), based in Kathmandu (Nepal).

In 1968 the League of Arab States created an Arab Permanent Committee on Human Rights, composed of representatives of the Member States, with an advisory and promotion role. Following the adoption of the Arab Charter on Human Rights (2004), which entered into force in 2008, an Arab Human Rights Committee was established in 2009 to oversee the implementation of the Charter, but no complaints mechanism is available.

It should be noted that International Human Rights Law aims at guaranteeing a minimum of protection and should not be invoked to justify not implementing higher national standards.

There are electronic mechanisms, easily accessible, for lodging complaints of human rights violations within the UN system and the regional systems.

International Human Rights Law has thus conferred on individuals status of international legal personality, when they can turn to international fora if their human rights are not respected.

International mechanisms for the protection of human rights are of last resort, however. Recourse to international bodies is subject to admissibility conditions, especially the exhaustion of remedies available under domestic legal systems, if they exist, are affordable and reliable.

The protection of human rights against their violation by non-State international actors, especially multinational corporations, has become more pressing with the expansion of Globalisation.

There are tens of thousands of Non-governmental Organisations, international and national, devoted to human rights, such as International Federation for Human Rights, Amnesty International, Human Rights Watch. They play an irreplaceable role, by *naming and shaming,* as well as an increasing role in the development of International Law as spokespersons of the civil society. An educated world public opinion is the ultimate protection of human rights.

- **Justiciability**

A general (customary) principle of justice is that the violation of a right must be remediable. Remedies include impartial investigation, cessation of the violation if it is ongoing, restitution, compensation, rehabilitation, guarantees of non-repetition, or otherwise.

When the victims of violation (or threat of violation) of their rights (or someone on their behalf) can submit a complaint to an independent and impartial instance, to repair (or to prevent) it, the right is said to be justiciable.

Justiciability, in a strict sense, is accomplished by Tribunals, which are the organs typically competent to give binding decisions based on laws and facts. In a broader sense, the mechanisms of justiciability include other entities with similar power or only powers of recommendation and mediation. Although the judicial route is, in principle, the most effective means of redress against human rights violations, what matters is that they are effectively repaired (or prevented), whatever the mechanisms, judicial or other.

The justiciability of economic, social and cultural rights was controversial for a long time, in the context of the Cold War, growing from the 1950s, which influenced the decision to adopt two International Covenants in 1952 (instead of just one, as the UN General Assembly had first decided). While Western countries (market economies) put first civil and political rights (the *blue* rights), the Eastern bloc of socialist/communist countries (centrally planned economies) gave priority to economic, social and cultural rights (the *red* rights). Many arguments are fallacious, and the controversy became legally groundless after the adoption, in 2008, of the Optional Protocol to the International Covenant on Economic, Social and Cultural Rights on a communications procedure.

There is not yet a World Court of Human Rights, although the idea goes back to the *travaux préparatoires* (drafting, legislative history) of the Universal Declaration and has recently been relaunched[30]. The International Court of Justice (United Nations), which only settles disputes between States and gives Advisory Opinions, pronounced several decisions relevant for the human rights protection. The jurisdiction of the International Criminal Court, established by the Rome Statute adopted on 17 July 1998 (entered into force on 1 July 2002), is limited to the most serious international crimes (genocide, crimes against humanity, war crimes, crimes of aggression), but there are the regional Courts abovementioned. The most comprehensive human rights international Case Law was pronounced by the organs of the European Convention on Human Rights (the European Court of Human Rights and the former European Commission of Human Rights).

The jurisprudence (interpretation of rules and following decisions) of Higher Courts, international and national, by fleshing out general, abstract norms, contributes significantly to the normative development of human rights. The same applies to the "quasi-jurisprudence" and General Comments or General Recommendations of the UN Committees, without forgetting the relevance notably of the Limburg Principles on the Implementation of the International Covenant on Economic, Social and Cultural Rights (1986), the Maastricht Guidelines on Violations of Economic, Social and Cultural Rights (1997) and the Maastricht Principles on Extraterritorial Obligations of States in the area of Economic, Social and Cultural Rights (2011).

1.1.6 Ethics of Human Rights

Axiology, Morals, Ethics – are terms belonging to the same semantic family.

Axiology is the philosophical discipline that studies values, in general, that is, what makes things desirable. Values are manifold: there are instrumental values, which are means for reaching other ones, such as wealth and power; other are both means and ends, such as health and knowledge; other ones are ends giving sense to, or alleviating, the human existence, such as happiness, beauty, justice: they are principally moral or ethical values.

Ethics and Morals are terms etymologically different (of Greek and Latin origin, respectively), but synonymous. Both refer to behaviours, customs and values that regulate individual and collective life. That is why they are terms often used indistinctly or redundantly, as when one says, "ethical and moral behaviour". Nevertheless, they may be distinguished. Some authors make the following distinction:

- Morals denotes the individual values or values common to a group or community, which are inculcated to its members as norms of good and evil, of right and wrong behaviour. So understood, the term has a particularistic connotation.

- Ethics is a theory or systematic reflection concerning morality, also called Moral Philosophy. So understood, the term has a universalistic scope and can also designate a moral normativity claiming cross-cultural validity. This is the case with Ethics of Human Rights (it is not usually said 'Morals of Human Rights').

The history of human rights is the history of the *invention* of Man by mans. Of the revelation of the *Human Being in human beings.* The Human Being is the ethical subject transcending the empirical subjects – ethnic, cultural, national, social, familial, psychological and other ones – with their roots, cradles, memberships, differences and other circumstances. The *ethical subject* stands for the field of values and the forum of conscience as the *epistemic subject* for the field of knowledge and the realm of science (as well as the *citizen* for the social diversity).

Human rights constitute an Ethics because their source and sense are the worth and dignity of the human person, whose absolute primacy they consecrate[31].

The Ethics of Human Rights concentrates the juice of the most Edenic fruits of the cultural plurality of the humankind, expressing the quintessence of the evolution of its conscience. It is an intercultural Ethics with juridical force and political, economic, pedagogical and other exigencies as to how every human being should be treated and should treat other human beings, by virtue of their equal worth and dignity. Adding a universal moral heritage to the genetic heritage of the human species and the cultural heritage of communities and persons, human rights vest every human being with a common ethical identity, making them citizens of the world. A Roman citizen could say in his defence: *Civis romanus sum!* (I'm a Roman citizen!). Now, a human being can claim everywhere: *Civis humanus sum!* (I'm a human citizen!)[32].

Here is the most profound and transcendent significance of the Ethics of Human Rights: The Human Being should be a *God* for human beings. His temple *sanctum sanctorum* (the most sacred place) is Human Dignity.

1.1.6.1 Human Dignity Principle

- **Origins**

Dignity is a term with many uses. It is applied not only to human beings but also to institutions, offices, professions, symbols, even to animals and plants.

The Human Dignity Principle has a plurality of cultural, religious, and philosophical roots.

Dignitas (dignity) meant, in ancient Roma, a hierarchical, privileged status, related to social origin or the exercise of public office, implying corresponding composure and deference. It could also be connected with personal virtue, in the Aristotelian sense (moral character or habit/willingness to act morally well).

Stoicism – a Philosophy originated in Athens of the 3rd century BC, according to which happiness lies in liberation from desires and passions that disturb self-control and inner peace – associated *dignitas hominis* (man's dignity) with the faculty of reason.

Following the Christian Theology, earthly creatures form a great chain where the status of each one is defined by its ontological distance from the divine Creator. Man's superiority derives from his likeness with God (*Imago Dei*), who created him with an immortal *soul*.

In the Renaissance (15th – 16th centuries), the most famous text on human dignity was *Oratio de Hominis Dignitate* (Oration on the Dignity of Man), by Giovanni Pico della Mirandola, published posthumously (1496), according to which the uniqueness of human beings consists in their ontological openness and freedom to choose what they want to be.

In the following centuries, the term 'dignity' kept, in general, a differentiating use: not an attribute of everyone, but only of a few.

... and Kant has come.

- **Kant**

Great ideas are like rivers with remote sources, with many tributaries. The most sublime moral idea – Human Dignity – flowed into the ocean of thought of Immanuel Kant (1724-1804). He is generally prized as the Philosopher of Human Dignity.

Kant 'liberated' human dignity from external (religious and metaphysical) foundations and gave it an immanent foundation – autonomy of will. His "Principle of Humanity" – namely: "Act in such a way that you treat humanity, both in your own person and in that of others, always, at the same time, as an end, never merely as a means" – became the Human Dignity Principle *par excellence.*

The fullness of the Kantian conception of human dignity may be summarised in this way: A human being possesses *intrinsic worth and dignity* because (s)he is a *rational being* capable of *freedom* and *morality* through the *autonomy of the will.* Human beings are therefore *ends in themselves* and, if they behave according to norms that could be valid for everyone, they become *universal legislators* and members of an *ideal realm of ends,* analogous to the realm of nature. The Dignity of Humanity calls for reciprocity and compassion – the ancient and universal commandment of the Golden Rule.

The Kantian vision of human dignity was the philosophical culmination of the historical *democratisation* of the aristocratic Roman *dignitas,* while retaining a sense of value and respect. Kant was the author of an ethical revolution which, in the 20th century, became a juridical revolution, inspiration for political revolutions.

- **Juridification**

The term 'human dignity' does not feature in the 18th century American and French Bills of Rights. It was in the 20th century that it entered progressively into the Constitutional and International Law, especially after World War II.

The internationalisation of human dignity has definitely begun with the UN Charter (1945) that proclaimed, "faith in fundamental human rights, in the dignity and worth of the human person" (Preamble), echoing in the Universal Declaration of Human Rights (1948), which refers to human dignity in Preamble and several Articles, becoming the source of its torrential expansion. In the International Bill of Human Rights, we find 14 references to human dignity and, if we turn to the other human rights treaties forming, with the 1966 Covenants, the Core International Human Rights Treaties, we find the term about 30 times more.

Surprisingly, the term 'human dignity' is not found in the European Convention on Human Rights, adopted "to take the first steps for the collective enforcement of certain of the rights stated in the Universal Declaration" (Preamble)[33]. It only appeared in 2002, in the Preamble to its Protocol 13 concerning the abolition of the death penalty as "essential for the protection of this right [to life] and for the full recognition of the inherent dignity of all human beings". However, "respect for human dignity and human freedom" is "the very essence of the Convention", as said the European Court of Human Rights (*Van Kück v. Germany* Application 35968/97, 12 June 2003, para. 69)[34]. The Court has referred to "human dignity" in more than one thousand judgments, especially in Cases related with Article 3 (Prohibition of torture) of the European Convention, but also with Article 2 (Right to life) and Article 4 (Prohibition of slavery and forced labour).

The German Constitution post-Nazism (*Grundgesetzt:* Basic Law, which came into effect on 23 May 1949)[35] has famously proclaimed: *Die Menschenwüde ist unantastbar* (Human dignity is intangible)[36]. This proclamation radiated to all continents. In the following *human dignity constitutional revolution,* after the new Constitutions of the countries defeated in the war – Japan (1947), Italy (1947), Germany (1949) – two decades stand out:

- 1970s, with the new Constitutions born from the fall of dictatorships: Greece (1975), Portugal (1976), Spain (1978)

- 1990s, with the Constitutions of the new countries of central and eastern Europe, after the Fall of the Berlin Wall (1989)

An example of the powerful resonance of the German proclamation is the Charter of Fundamental Rights of the European Union, which devotes its Title I to "Dignity" and whose Article 1 (Human dignity) states simply: "Human dignity is inviolable. It must be respected and protected."[37]

The Basic Law of the Federal Republic of Germany (1949) and the Constitution of the Republic of South Africa (1996) are among the most human dignity and rights heavy, and this is not by chance: they were reactions to somewhat similar morally devastating backgrounds: Nazism and Apartheid, respectively – political regimes of principled denial of the common human dignity[38]. Both Constitutions begin with long catalogues of human rights[39], shielded by special clauses[40].

Although the Basic Law only mentions human dignity in Article 1.1, it is a term and a value ubiquitous in its Case Law. For instance, the German Federal Constitutional Court said (*BVerfG, 15* February 2006, para. 119)[41]: "Human life is the vital basis of human dignity as the essential constitutive principle, and as the supreme value, of the Constitution (see BVerfGE 39, 1 (42); 72, 105 (115); 109, 279 (311))."

Human dignity features more times in the South African Constitution[42]. The first of its "Founding Provisions" (Chapter 1, 1.a) reads: "Human dignity, the achievement of equality and the advancement of human rights and freedoms." Its "Bill of Rights" (Chapter 2) begins by stating (7.1): "This Bill of Rights is a cornerstone of democracy in South Africa. It enshrines the rights of all people in our country and affirms the democratic values of human dignity, equality and freedom." It also states (10): "Everyone has inherent dignity and the right to have their dignity respected and protected."

The US Constitution doesn't mention human dignity, but the Federal Supreme Court has invoked it hundreds of times, by interpreting various of the constitutional Amendments.

What is *human dignity?*

During the *travaux préparatoires* of the Universal Declaration (1947-1948), it was not possible to reach a consensus on the foundation of human dignity and rights. The issue gave rise to one of the hottest debates within the UN General Assembly Third Committee, in the autumn of 1948, between proponents of a reference to a Creator and proponents of a reference to Nature. Since no agreement was possible, both words were eventually avoided. The sole indication is laid down in Article 1 (that reproduces almost literally the first paragraph of the Preamble of the American Declaration of the Rights and Duties of Man, adopted some months before), following which human beings "are endowed with reason and conscience". However, no agreement was reached on "the origin of man's reason and conscience" (A/C.3/SR.99)[43].

Human dignity was then the Universal Sign – a kind of *Floating Signifier*[44] – welcoming the cultural, religious and ideological heterogeneity of the representatives of the UN Member States, but all having a common heartbreaking sentiment: human dignity is what the Nazi extermination camps and their gas chambers trampled on in an appalling scale.

During the following decades, the impressive legal and jurisprudential expansion of the Human Dignity Principle is attributed, in part, to its vagueness. It has been called *empty shell, empty placeholder*, a term *passe-partout* (catch-all), even *legoland, smokescreen,* ending up being a *two-edged sword,* and its uses have been said to be a *conceptual chaos,* a *cacophony*. Indeed, it's a term whose invocation may not always avoid the Scylla of abstraction or the Charybdis of trivialisation…

Repeated attempts have been made to identify a core content of "human dignity" and to categorise the variety of its jurisprudential uses, but it remains, paradoxically, a foundation lacking to be founded...

- **Conceptualisation**

This author has proposed, in other publications, the conception of human dignity that will be synthesized and improved under the following headings:

- *Human dignity is the Principle and the sense of human rights*
- *Human dignity is an ethical value with a genetic foundation*
- *Human dignity consists in the species' perfectibility calling for its members' perfecting*
- *Human dignity is essential-absolute and existential-relative*
- *Human dignity is inviolable and indisposable*
- *Human dignity is vulnerable and variable*
- *Human dignity is the Great Sign of recognition of belonging to the human species*
- *Human dignity is the Principle and the sense of human rights*

A preliminary doctrinal question is whether human dignity should be considered a right or a principle. It already sparked a debate in the course of the preparatory works of the Universal Declaration. Subsequently, in International and Constitutional Law, human dignity is invoked in preambular texts, or in connection with particular human rights, or as a right, or as the foundation of all human rights. When it is said to be a right, it is not put on an equal footing as other rights, however[45].

Between human dignity and rights there is a circular relation: respecting human dignity is to respect human rights, whose source is the human dignity. They are like the two sides of a medal – the medal of *being human* – so that human dignity amounts to the *ursprungsrecht* (the right-source): *ein Recht, Rechte zu haben* (a right to have rights). It is a kind of *Grundnorm* (foundational norm) – the supreme value[46].

The Committee on Economic, Social and Cultural Rights said, in its General Comment 13 (E/C.12/1999/10, para. 41)[47], that human dignity is "the fundamental guiding principle of International Human Rights Law enshrined in the Preambles to the Universal Declaration of Human Rights and both Covenants". The Declaration and Program of Action of Vienna (1993)[48] has reaffirmed that "all human rights derive from the dignity and worth inherent in the human person" (Preamble).

Thus, human dignity should be considered rather as the Principle of human rights – immanent and transcendent. Immanent, i.e. without metaphysical, religious or social foundations, and transcendent because, although each right is inherent in human dignity, there is dignity without rights: it precedes them, when they cannot yet be exercised, and subsists when one loses the capacity to exercise them. Nor is it reducible to the sum of the rights recognised in a given historical epoch.

It is as a principle that human dignity can serve as criterion for resolving conflicts between dignity and rights, between individual rights, between rights of different persons, between two positions of dignity, between individual dignity and collective dignity.

Human dignity has become a higher jurisprudential principle, leitmotif of the political rhetoric, flag of all causes and struggles against oppression and injustice. In Ukraine, in 2014, there was a "Revolution of Dignity".

Human Dignity is, therefore, more fully understood as *Principle* of foundation, interpretation, application and expansion of human rights.

- *Human dignity is an ethical value with a genetic foundation*

The *passion* of International Human Rights Law is "the dignity and worth of the human person". If they are not redundant terms, 'dignity' is taken as the foundation of 'worth'. If so, the question remains: What is the foundation of dignity?

If we change the words' sequence – "worth and dignity" – it could be distinguished between worth as *genetic value* and dignity as *ethical value,* the former being the foundation of the latter. This raises the anthropologically essential question: What are the attributes or faculties distinguishing the human species from other ones? What does it mean to be human? What is Man?

Over the centuries, there have been many answers. The idea of *human nature* has oscillated between two poles: immutability (it is a *given*) and mutability (it is a *becoming*). At present, it can be argued that the *humanness* is a creation of an evolutionary chain of bio-cultural processes of interaction between bipedalism, freeing of hands, increased volume of the brain, life in groups, development of the symbolic function. It emerged from the brain neuroplasticity that is the material basis of the mental semioticity, generating rationality and creativity, driven by emotions, which raised human evolution to a higher level.

- *Neuroplasticity* is the most extraordinary property of the human brain. It consists in the electrochemical dynamism of its neurons, giving it an inexhaustible potential to respond to all stimuli, internal and external, causing structural and functional changes. It forms synaptic networks underlying neuronal maps that are reflected in mental images.

- *Semioticity* is the generating function of mental images. The semiotic aptitude is a power of creation, utilisation and interpretation of symbols or signs, whose most humanly specific and powerful expression is language – a new form of communication and relationship. Man is "a speaking animal". Semioticity may be considered the 'organ' of rationality.

- *Rationality* is the faculty that allows the detachment from the sensible variety of the concrete, immediate world, through abstraction, conceptualisation, reflection, imagination. It is the emanation of a process of bio-cultural co-evolution, opening human beings to a temporality that transcends the present, made of past and future, memory and project. A power of dissatisfaction, self-determination, transformation.

- *Creativity* is the new world of the liberty of rationality. It is at the origin of the fabulous cultural diversity of the human species and of new forms of civilisational self-regulation, through moral, intellectual, legal, political, economic, technological, artistic, invention. Morality is the most *immortalising* fruit of creativity, because moral values are *symbolic prostheses* necessary for the coexistence, perfecting and destiny of a species whose *humanity* is a fragile stratum of its animality.

- *Emotions* are complex reactions with three components, according to neuroscientist Antonio Damasio: a mental state, a physiological change and an impulse to act. There are natural emotions and social emotions such as compassion, admiration, guilt, shame, pride, jealousy, envy, some of which seem to be exclusively human. Emotions have a cognitive and evaluative, positive or negative, adaptive value, generating *somatic markers* that influence many of our decisions and behaviours. They are the source of moral principles, of what is humanly unique, probably inaccessible to any *cyborg*...

Human nature being a seamless bio-cultural creation, the old nature-culture, innate-acquired controversy, has become obsolete, as well as the opposition reason-emotion and other similar dualisms. There is a permanent interaction within and with the exterior of the organism, the reality of which does not diminish the sublimity of the fruits of creativity such as Morals, Art and Science.

Given the interface-nature of semioticity – between neuroplasticity and rationality – this is probably the most profound and far-reaching definition of the human species: *Man is a symbolic or semiotic animal.*

Yet it is not enough to be genetically human to be treated and to behave humanely. Human dignity also needs intersubjective, ethical recognition. *Re-cognition* is like knowledge to the second power: *seeing* beyond what one sees. *Ethical recognition* means to see in each human being, first and foremost, an equal and treating him or her as one wants to be treated (Golden Rule). "The essential is invisible to the eye" – says the fox of *The Little Prince*[49].

Without recognition of human dignity and rights, one can enter a gas chamber, but one does not enter the House of Humanity. Nazism is an ideology of non-recognition of the common human dignity – that is the least that can be said. The rest is unspeakable. It is Auschwitz, symbol of the Nazi *entwürdigung* (annihilation of dignity).

The double foundation – genetic and ethical – of human dignity is indicated in the Universal Declaration on the Human Genome and Human Rights adopted by UNESCO in 1997[50] and endorsed by the UN General Assembly, that begins by stating (Article 1): "The *human genome* underlies the fundamental unity of all members of the *human family*, as well as the *recognition* of their inherent *dignity* and *diversity*." (italics added)

- *Human dignity consists in the species' perfectibility calling for its members' perfecting*

The ongoing neurobiological revolution, since the 1990s – the 'brain decade', boosted by new non-invasive techniques allowing to study the brain in operation, through a variety of brain images (SPECT, MRI, PET, fMRI) – confirms that the most profoundly distinctive biological attribute of the human species is *perfectibility*, with the inherent need for *perfecting*. The German Federal Constitutional Court equated human life, human dignity and perfectibility when it said in *BVerfGE 39, 1, 1975*

(*Schwangerschaftsabbruch* I)[51]: "Where human life exists, human dignity is present to it [...]. The potential faculties present in the human being from the beginning suffice to establish human dignity." (para. 122)

The seeds of the higher aptitudes contained in the human genome are the raw material for perfecting. It is deemed that only 10% of our nearly 100 billion neurons are interconnected at birth. The other 90% connexions depend on multiple existential factors. As reads Article 3 of the abovementioned UNESCO Declaration:

> The human genome, which by its nature evolves, is subject to mutations. It contains potentialities that are expressed differently according to each individual's natural and social environment, including the individual's state of health, living conditions, nutrition, and education.

Consequently, members of the human species are not born fully human. Besides recognition, they need perfecting that, since perfectibility means educability, is accomplished through education.

- *Human dignity is essential-absolute and existential-relative*

The essential-absolute human dignity is meant by the Kantian Principle of Humanity commanding never to treat a human being merely as object but always also as an end, because endowed with the aptitude for autonomy and free rational agency. This is the *Objektformel* (formula-object) applied by the German Federal Constitutional Court[52]. It has become a kind of *constitutional categoric imperative*[53].

However, a decent and meaningful life requires a minimum of wellbeing and participation in cultural, social and political life, without which human dignity is an abstraction. This is an existential-relative vision of human dignity, because it involves the satisfaction of rights whose scope is jurisprudentially variable[54].

In sum: The human dignity is absolute-relative, as it concerns life, freedom and justice. It is about power and empowerment[55].

- *Human dignity is inviolable and inalienable*

Human dignity is inviolable (intangible) in a descriptive and prescriptive sense:

- Human dignity is inviolable in a descriptive sense to the extent that, given its genetic foundation, a human being never loses it. The victims of the Nazi extermination camps died with their human dignity, which has survived them in their ashes, deeds, words, especially in the memory of their beloved.

- Human dignity is inviolable in a prescriptive sense because it is an absolute command, a categoric imperative[56].

Human dignity is inalienable (indisposable) because it is not just an individual good, but one common to the whole species. For instance, nobody is free to sell himself or herself as a slave (it would be a contradiction) and, if someone is involuntarily enslaved, (s)he retains his or her human dignity. There are not human rights against human dignity. It must prevail over individual autonomy, if necessary.

- *Human dignity is vulnerable and variable*

Nevertheless, human dignity is vulnerable and variable as objective genetic and intersubjective ethical value[57].

The human dignity is vulnerable, as objective genetic value, because the human genome may be endangered by anomalies or henceforth altered through biotechnologies. And life may be annihilated by wars, death penalty, homicide, suicide. It is variable firstly because the liberty of rationality is not operating ab initio (from the beginning of life) and is lost in the case of mental degeneration.

The human dignity is vulnerable and variable as intersubjective ethical value, in several ways, including the following:

- Human dignity and rights are not respected when human beings are victims of physical and/or psychological cruelties, misery, disease, and each time they are treated simply as 'objects', 'instruments'.

- Human dignity is also undermined when honour and personal reputation are attacked, defamed, with reflexes in the sense of self-worth and self-esteem and possible material losses[58].

- Because human beings live in families and communities, discrimination, segregation and marginalisation of the groups to which they belong also affect the sense of dignity of their members[59]. And if they generate delinquent and violent behaviour, they are threats for the safety and well-being of the whole society[60].

- The perfecting of each human being may be hindered by cultural, social, economic, political and other conditions, which explain different incarnations and expressions of the equal dignity.

- Although all members of the human species have absolute dignity, regardless of what they do, individual choices and behaviours may be unworthy, arousing disapproval or even sanctions (it is the Kantian distinction between *inner worth* and *moral worth*). On the contrary, people can distinguish themselves by their virtues and other merits, arousing respect and admiration that magnify their dignity and human dignity in general.

- *Human dignity is the Great Sign of recognition of belonging to the human species*

The Universal Declaration of Human Rights begins with "the recognition of the inherent dignity and of the equal and inalienable rights of all members of the human family" (first preambular paragraph). Therefore, who belongs to the *human family* is endowed with human dignity, whatever their gender, age, capacities, virtues or crimes, including unborn life, parts of the human body and deceased persons[61].

Human dignity is embodied in faces of happiness and suffering, in figures of genius and dementia, in venerated saints and sinister criminals. The executors of the Nazi hallucination had the human dignity they did not recognise in their victims.

The still inevitable wars for the values of Civilisation are not won with the barbarity of those who vilify them. Barbarity begets barbarity... The most powerful and sacred weapon against barbarity is pity for Humanity.

- *Last remarks*

- As there is no precise juridical definition of human dignity, a violations approach prevails, but identifying violations implies some representation of what being human means. In this regard, the famous words of Justice Stewart come to mind, in a Case concerning the public exhibition of an allegedly obscene film, concurring with the US Supreme Court decision that the film was not obscene. In his opinion, the applicable criminal laws are constitutionally limited to "hard core pornography". He did not attempt to define it, and perhaps could he not succeed, "But I know it when I see it" (*Jacobellis v. Ohio, 378 U.S. 184 (1964)*)[62].

- All human rights are inherent in human dignity, but not all are equally close to it. Many treaties allow for reservations and declarations of interpretation, when States sign or ratify them. Implementation of many of them may be progressive. Most human rights may be restricted or even suspended, under certain conditions. The core of human dignity are rights most close to the physical, moral and psychological integrity of the human person, namely: right to life and to freedom from torture and cruel, inhuman or degrading treatment or punishment, as well as from slavery and servitude.

- As human dignity is both the dignity of the species and of each of its members, this dual dimension gives to the Human Dignity Principle a function both of protection and of limitation of the autonomy. If individual behaviours clash with collective representations or interests, conflicting interpretations raise more or less controversial *hard cases*, such as abortion, euthanasia or assisted suicide, lifetime imprisonment, death penalty, prostitution, pornography, homosexuality, same-sex unions. Among the hardest ones are bestiality or zoophilia, generally qualified as sexual behaviour *contra natura* (contrary to nature).

- Human Dignity is the most brilliant star in the human rights firmament, the highest lighthouse in the ocean of the human species' indefinite destiny. It lies at the heart of Human Rights Philosophy and is the spinal column of International Human Rights Law. Human dignity has become the supreme moral value of a New Constitutionalism, the axiological core of the Rule of Law, the *soul* of a Law of Humanity in *statu nascendi* (in gestation).

- An unpleasant outcome of the proposed conceptualisation is the following: We live in times of mental transition between the belief in a *human essence* – immortal *soul* or innate *reason* – and the science that humans are bio-cultural creatures, which dissolve with death…

- Anyway, looking at the savage past of the species and the savagery remaining in our sight, we must conclude: The Human Dignity Principle is the quintessence of Civilisation.

- In sum: Human Dignity is a *natural attribute*, a *moral status*, and a *personal responsibility*.

1.1.6.2 Other Principles

The Constitutional Court of Colombia said that equality is "a principle, value and right, i.e. it enjoys a triple legal identity" (*T-363/16*, para. 9)[63]. It is a moral value legally protected as human right that is a cornerstone of the architecture of International Human Rights Law. Such may be also considered, in addition to the Human Dignity Principle, the following values-rights-principles constituent of the Ethics of Human Rights: Life, Liberty, Diversity, Non-discrimination, with the correspondent Responsibility. Their preeminence is very briefly justified next.

- **Life**

Life is *sine qua non,* i.e. the biological condition of having rights, its loss being irreparable[64]. From this perspective, the *sanctity of life* is the supreme right. Life and human dignity are the double source of all human rights[65].

The right to life is not absolute, however. International Human Rights Law still admits the death penalty (tough Protocols aiming at its abolition have been adopted), and other intentional (but not arbitrary) deprivations of life are permitted (killing in self-defense or in a war scenario). And there are situations in which one risks, or even sacrifices, one's life for values considered superior.

The right to life (or, more rigorously, the right to live) should not be restrictively understood as only right to biological, animal existence. When human life is exhausted in the urgency of daily survival, to defend against real threats or to satisfy vital needs, human beings live and may behave simply like animals...

Nowadays, the right to life has transversal content, jurisprudentially developed by higher Courts such as the Supreme Court of India, the Constitutional Court of South Africa, the Inter-American Court of Human Rights, giving it a normative density with three main dimensions:

- Protection against deprivation of *biological life*
- Assuring the basic conditions for a *human life*
- Accomplishing a *life project*

The Universal Declaration of Human Rights proclaims in its Article 1: "All human beings are born free and equal in dignity and rights." Equality and Liberty are twin sisters – older daughters of Human Dignity.

- **Equality**

The Principle of Equality is the basis of the edifice of International Human Rights Law.

All kinds of racism reduce human beings to their ethnic look. All forms of culturalism reduce human beings to their cultural clothing. Any reductionism undermines human dignity, the fullness of which includes the equality, diversity and uniqueness of human beings. When *ethnicity* and *culturality* prevail over *ethicity,* when an *Aryan dignity* appropriates *human dignity,* when *religiosity* trumps *humanity,* any barbarity is possible…

Equality means, of course, moral equality, equality before the law, equal protection of the law, equality of rights, as well as right to all that is necessary for "larger freedom" or liberty (Preamble to the Universal Declaration).

- **Liberty**

Liberty or freedom[66] is a *sacré-mot* (sacred word) of International Human Rights Law. It is far more recurrent than 'equality' and even much more than 'dignity'[67]. Liberty is the *elixir* of humanisation.

Human rights are conditions or modalities of liberty/freedom, in particular the right to privacy, which has an unusual breadth in the Case Law of the European Court of Human Rights. Without ever defining its full scope, the Court has given the concept of "private life" a dynamic, evolving, open and flexible content. An openness and flexibility enabling it to adapt the right to private life, interpreted on a case-by-case basis, with sensitivity, to cultural, social, economic, technological and legal changes, including in it elements not covered by the rights recognised in the European Convention on Human Rights.

Liberty is a factor of diversity.

- **Diversity**

People tend to believe in the superiority of their own culture, but Civilisation is a creation of the cultural diversity.

In 2001, was adopted the UNESCO Universal Declaration on Cultural Diversity. Introducing it, the Director-General (then Koïchiro Matsuura) wrote[68]:

> This Declaration, which sets against inward-looking fundamentalism the prospect of a more open, creative and democratic world, is now one of the founding texts of the new ethics promoted by UNESCO in the early twenty-first century. My hope is that one day it may acquire the same force as the Universal Declaration of Human Rights.

The Declaration recalls (Article 4): "No one may invoke cultural diversity to infringe upon human rights guaranteed by International Law, nor to limit their scope."

Perhaps the most complex issue raised by human rights concerns the relationship between their universality and culturality, i.e. between the abstract Human Being and the concrete human beings. Because human rights do not exist in a cultural and social *vacuum*, International Human Rights Law is not 'culture-blind'. Much less so in the era of Globalisation that has given the world's cultural diversity unprecedented visibility.

Humankind is not a Palace of Mirrors, indefinitely reflecting each other, but rather a Symphony of Differences. As human beings are born in communities whose cultures form a collective identity transfused into individual identities, the human dignity has many cribs, many bodies, many faces, many voices, many manifestations. Beliefs, clothing, music, dances, are expressions of the common heritage of the human diversity. Every fundamentalism is hostile to the liberty of diversity.

Human rights are compatible with every difference not incompatible with their values. Their universal language may be *spoken* in 'cultural dialects'. There is a right to be different (see 2.3.2).

If the most visible diversity of human beings is that of their appearance, the deepest one is the invisible, psychological diversity: differences of life stories, inner worlds, needs, possibilities, desires, dreams ...

- **Non-discrimination**

The Principle of Non-discrimination is a corollary of the Principles of Equality, Liberty and Diversity.

The UN Charter (1945), which mentions human rights seven times, uses the expression "without distinction" four times. The Universal Declaration of 1948 states the principle of non-discrimination immediately in Article 2 and also enshrines it in Article 7. The 1966 International Covenants devote general provisions to it in Articles 2 and 3. It crosses International Human Rights Law and is addressed by several specific instruments. For example, it is the subject of Protocol 12 (2000) to the European Convention on Human Rights (which dedicates Article 14 to it), thus extending its protection to the field of economic, social and cultural rights. It has become Customary International Law and *Jus Cogens*.

Discrimination consists of acts or omissions that affect the respect for the equal dignity and rights. It may be *de jure* (legal) or *de facto* (real), active or passive, direct or indirect, multiple and cumulative.

In International Human Rights Law, we find the terms "discrimination" and "distinction", but the former is the most rigorous, as the achievement of equality may imply distinctions. Indeed, while forbidding unequal treatment of equal situations, the principle of non-discrimination legitimises unequal treatment of unequal situations, when it is necessary to give more to those who most need, for creating conditions of equality. It is a "positive discrimination" (reverse discrimination or affirmative action) that should be objectively justified and temporary, in order to have no effect of discrimination against third parties or even to revert to stigmatization of its beneficiaries.

- **Responsibility**

The human rights discourse is sometimes blamed for individualism, forgetting duties. The debate goes back to the drafting of the 1789 French Declaration and revived during the legislative history of the 1948 Universal Declaration. However, the idea of including duties in it was not welcomed at the time, because the urgency was *to cry* rights that had been so extremely violated during World War II. Nevertheless, duties are not absent from the Declaration: "Everyone has duties to the community in which alone the free and full development of his personality is possible." (Article 29.1) There are many references to duties in International Human Rights Law. For example, in the title of the American Declaration of the Rights and Duties of Man (1948) and in the African Charter on Human and Peoples' Rights (1981, Articles 27-29).

Human rights are ethically individualistic, by definition – that is, they are recognised to protect and promote the worth, dignity and liberty of each human person – but this does not mean, in no way, that individuals are envisaged as isolated, abstract entities. The principle of reciprocity is inherent to the concept of human rights. Rights and duties are like the two sides of a coin: if everyone has rights, each one has duties. They are duties to oneself, to others, to the common Humanity, including generations to come.

At present, the term 'responsibility' is preferred, because it does not have the moralistic connotations of 'duty'. Each and every one is responsible for his or her own dignity and for the dignity of the species, which are inseparable: Whoever does not respect his or her own dignity offends the dignity of all human beings, and whoever does not respect the dignity of others offends his or her own dignity.

1.1.6.3 Ethics of Recognition

Recognition may be considered a vital need and the most profound desire of a human being. Even if it's sometimes recognition by someone who mistreats us or just by a dog or a cat...[69]

Recognition is a kaleidoscopic phenomenon. There are multiple expressions and institutions of recognition in personal and social relations. Daily life is a theatre, at a variety of stages, of scenes and games of tacit demands, expectations, or declared and generalised competition and struggles for recognition, variable in their dramaticity, morality and geniality.

Since the 1980s, 'recognition' has become a sign-flag of struggles of numerous groups who feel discriminated against because of their ethnic, religious, gender, sexual orientation and other differences. The heuristic power of the idea of recognition has been rediscovered and attracted a great deal of interest in the social sciences field, giving rise to programmes of transdisciplinary studies and debates.

Recognition is generally associated with valorisation. The value of human beings is assessed according to:

- Their being (ethical-legal value)
- Their doing (instrumental-functional value)
- Their having (economic value, source of social status)
- Their looking (erotic-aesthetical value of seduction-attraction)

Look, *figure,* is a value that largely escapes individual will. It is erotic and aesthetic in nature, consisting of a kind of bodily capital that interacts with other values. Economic goods, earned or inherited, always confer social status. Each human being is also valued for what they do, with possible social recognition that can bring symbolic and material rewards. It is, however, as a *human being* that everyone holds an unconditional *right to recognition.*

We already know the ethical significance of the idea of *recognition*. It is not surprising, therefore, that it has substantial normative weight in various fields of Law, in particular in Philosophy of Law, Civil Law, International Law, but principally International Human Rights Law. In its treaties, States Parties *recognise* human dignity and rights.

Here, then, is a possible definition:

The Ethics of Human Rights is an Ethics of the Recognition of Human Dignity as a Principle-Right to have Rights, which are fundamentally the Rights-Principles of Life, Equality, Liberty, Diversity, Non-discrimination, with the inherent Responsibility.

1.1.6.4 Ethics of the Humanity

The values and ideas improving the human condition begin to be in the minority.

The progress of Civilisation – moral, intellectual, artistic, political, economic, technological… – results from collective struggles and is protagonised by exceptional human beings: sages, creators, heroes, prophets, visionaries, martyrs … spokespersons and symbols of peoples' conscience, aspirations and geniality, as were the Big Five who have most influenced the drafting of the 1948 Universal Declaration – Eleanor Roosevelt (EUA), René Cassin (France), Charles Malik (Lebanon), Peng Chun Chang (Chine) and John P. Humphrey (Canada).

The Universal Declaration of Human Rights is an alchemy of intercultural and transtemporal moral values crystallized in the depths of human conscience. It was the beginning of the passage from Morals to Law of a set of values constituting a universal meta-morality, founded on the value and dignity of every human being, so that the "barbarous acts which have outraged the conscience of mankind" (second paragraph of the Preamble to the Declaration), committed during World War II, never happen again.

The Universal Declaration was compared to the Ten Commandments during its drafting. Eleanor Roosevelt, President of the Human Rights Commission that drafted it, said, addressing the UN General Assembly the day before its proclamation: "This Declaration of Human Rights may well become the international Magna Carta of all men everywhere."[70] Later, U. Thant (UN Secretary-General from 1962 to 1971) called it the Magna Carta of Mankind.

The universal ethical significance of human rights has been recalled again and again by the International Community. For instance:

- In 1968, the International Conference on Human Rights (Tehran) adopted a Resolution (XX) on "Education of youth in the respect for human rights and fundamental freedoms"[71] in which it affirmed "that the principles set forth in the Universal Declaration of Human Rights represent ethics common to all members of the international community" (Preamble).

- The Recommendation on Education for International Understanding and Co-operation and Peace and Education relating to Human Rights and Fundamental Freedoms (UNESCO, 1974, revised in 2023, now titled: Recommendation on Education for Peace and Human Rights, International Understanding, Cooperation, Fundamental Freedoms, Global Citizenship and Sustainable Development)[72] recommended to Member States (33.a): "provide teachers with motivations for their subsequent work: commitment to the ethics of human rights and to the aim of changing society, so that human rights are applied in practice".

- In 2008, the UN General Assembly stated in a Resolution on the "Sixtieth Anniversary of the Universal Declaration of Human Rights" (A/RES/63/116)[73]: "In an ever-changing world, the Universal Declaration of Human Rights remains a relevant ethical compass that guides us in addressing the challenges we face today."

The Parliament of the World's Religions (1993), recalling the 1948 Universal Declaration, adopted a Declaration on "Towards a Global Ethic"[74].

The foundation of the superior legitimacy of the Ethics of Human Rights lies in a *Great Consensus* that is a double Historical Consensus:

- *Moral consensus* of religious traditions and philosophical wisdom (Hinduism, Buddhism, Confucianism, Judaism, Christianity, Islamism, Stoicism, etc.), converging in the Golden Rule as a principle of reciprocity and compassion.

- *Legal consensus* written in the Universal Declaration of Human Rights as a "common understanding", amplified in many other instruments forming International Human Rights Law.

The *Great Consensus* underlying the Ethics of Human Rights is about "the supreme value of the human person", as wrote Hernán Santa Cruz, Chilean member of the drafting Sub-Committee of the Universal Declaration[75]:

> I perceived clearly that I was participating in a truly significant historic event in which a consensus had been reached as to the supreme value of the human person, a value that did not originate in the decision of a worldly power, but rather in the fact of existing – which gave rise to the inalienable right to live free from want and oppression and to fully develop one's personality.

The *Great Consensus* may be read in the light of Kant's Categorical Imperative. Its universality is ethically qualified by the Principle of Humanity. Moreover, the *common understanding* of the Universal Declaration may be interpreted as analogous to the Kantian *ideal realm of ends*.

Consequently, the *Great Consensus* shaping the Ethics of Human Rights is a virtuous one because it is based on the worth and dignity of the human person. Its legitimacy is above the occasional power of sinister majorities or minorities who arrogate to themselves the right to decide what is true or false, virtue or vice, beautiful or ugly, how everyone should think and behave, what is sexually permitted or forbidden, or even how to dress or to cut hair. It is the values of the *ethical democracy* that alone legitimise the *political democracies*. The ethical principle and the democratic principle are two pillars of the Rule of Law. Hitler became Chancellor of Germany 'democratically'[76].

The Ethics of Human Rights comprises five dimensions:

- *Vertical dimension*, concerning the relation between each State and all persons under its jurisdiction.

- *Horizontal dimension,* concerning inter-State relations, inter-individual relations and relations between individuals and other private actors.

- *Self-referential dimension,* concerning the relation of human beings and of the species with their own dignity.

- *Environmental dimension,* concerning the relationship between human beings and nature in general.

- *Intergenerational dimension,* concerning the relationship between present and future generations.

The Ethics of Human Rights may be more broadly represented as a Palace of Values: human dignity is the foundation; equality, liberty and diversity are the columns; non-discrimination is the dome; the variety of human rights are the salons, intercommunicating; tolerance, responsibility and solidarity are the gardens; democracy, development and peace are the oxygen, the bread and the music of the survival and wellbeing of the species living there; but it might get fatally damaged if the enchanted wood surrounding is ill-treated and the arches of the heritage of its natural, genetic and cultural treasures are not preserved.

The US Declaration of Independence (The unanimous Declaration of the thirteen United States of America, 4 July 1776)[77] proclaimed (italics added): "We hold these truths to be self-evident, that all men are created equal, that they are endowed by their *Creator* with certain unalienable Rights, that among these are Life, Liberty and the pursuit of Happiness." The French Declaration of the Rights of Man and the Citizen (26 August 1789)[78] referred (italics added) to "the natural, unalienable, and *sacred rights* of man" (Preamble). The UN Charter[79] proclaims – and the 1948 Universal Declaration recalls (italics added) – "*faith* in fundamental human rights, in the dignity and worth of the human person, in the equal rights of men and women and of nations large and small" (Preamble).

The Ethics of Human Rights has become the Common Temple of the *secular faith* of the Rule of Law[80]. And as human dignity will probably never be definitively protected and enhanced, the Human Rights Temple is an endless building, open to the *Possible* as the ethical *locus* of the undefined human perfectibility...

1.1.7 Revolution of Human Rights

Revolution is a frequent term in human rights literature.

Two culminating moments in the modern and contemporary history of human rights were the great 18th century Revolutions – the American Revolution and the French Revolution. And three documents should be highlighted:

- Declaration of the Rights of Man and the Citizen
  Decreed at the beginning of the French Revolution by the Constituent Assembly on 26 August 1789.

- Universal Declaration of Human Rights
  Proclaimed by the UN General Assembly on 10 December 1948.

- Convention on the Rights of the Child
  Adopted by the UN General Assembly on 20 November 1989.

The Universal Declaration of 1948 is the most symbolic document of the Revolution of Human Rights, which is compendiated in the first sentence of its Article 1: "All human beings are born free and equal in dignity and rights."

In 1998 – the year of the 50th anniversary of the Universal Declaration – the UN Secretary-General (at the time Kofi Annan), addressing the Annual Conference organised by the UN Department of Public Information (DPI) and NGOs, affirmed: "There is no turning back in the revolution of human rights."[81]

The Revolution of Human Rights has had repercussions in all domains of individual, social and international life, especially the following:

- Recognition of the ethical-juridical primacy of the Individual
- Refoundation of the International Law
- Renovation of the Constitutional Law
- Reconstruction of the Rule of Law
- Dawn of a Law of Humanity

The recognition and proclamation of *human rights* have been a gigantic civilisational step, jumping over the abyss where the human species was almost falling, in the first half of the 1940s. Nevertheless, contempt and violations of human rights keep daily an extremely shocking reality and will remain the overwhelming picture of the world for an unpredictably long time. This may be deeply disturbing and depressing ... However, the world being as it still is, a more positive attitude is asking: How would it be without the proclamation of the Universal Declaration of Human Rights?

Torture and some kinds of discrimination were morally and legally accepted until relatively recent times. Recognition of the rights of women and children, as well as of the rights concerning sexuality, are recent breakthroughs. If it was possible to advance so much during so few decades, in spite of everything, we must be idealistic, but realistic, without being pessimistic: The Revolution of Human Rights is a daily, individual, collective, struggle, maybe endless...

The most decisive front of the Revolution of Human Rights is the Revolution of the Rights of the Child.

1.2 Rights of the Child

The historiography of childhood is a relatively recent field of research. Its origins are generally associated with two pioneering works: *L'enfant et la vie familiale sous l'Ancien Régime* (Philippe Ariès, 1960: Centuries of Childhood: A Social History of Family Life, 1965) and *History of Childhood* (Lloyd deMause, 1974).

Beginning in the 1980s, new research called some of their conclusions into question. A subject of contention has been, in particular, the absence – or not – of the "feeling of childhood" and of parents' love for their children before modern times. The *Black Legend* (negative narrative) now has the competition of a *White Legend* (positive narrative), according to which in all eras there were positive feelings towards children and manifestations of parental affection for their children. The controversies should take into account the following:

- *Childhood* is a biological fact, but *child* and *family* are largely cultural and social definitions. The diversity of children's condition may not allow generalisations.

- The historiography of childhood has a problem of sources: they are not abounding and are mainly indirect, even more so regarding the lower social classes. And it is normal that new data could relativise previous conclusions.

- The history of childhood cannot be isolated from cultural, social, family, etc. contexts. Its realities could not help but be grim in times dominated by the struggle for survival, high infant mortality, low life expectancy, violent customs, widespread discrimination against women and girls, etc. This explains, for example, the 'normality' of infanticide and exposure and abandonment of newborns, which fed the slave trade.

The history of childhood is not, therefore, a black canvas with white dots, nor a white canvas with black dots. It is crossed by the ambivalence of children' representation, status and treatment by adults. Nevertheless, a pessimistic mindset has prevailed so far, underlying the lasting violence over children – historical paradigm of discrimination and oppression. The misfortune of childhood is a frequent inspiration in literature, especially children's literature.

Here is a possible schematic periodisation of the evolution of the representation, status and treatment of children:

- o *Ignorance* of the value of infancy and despise of children, regarded as inferior human beings and property of their progenitors (for millennia). The Roman Law of the XII Tables (c. 450 BC), allowing the *pater familias* (father) a *vitae necisque potestas* (power of life and death) reflects the mindset of that night of times.

- *Knowledge of* the specificity of childhood and dawn of a new sensitivity regarding children as developing human beings, arousing feelings of compassion and love and demanding protection and care (since modern times). This evolution gained expression, to a certain extent, in the French Napoleonic Code (1804).
- *Recognition* of the child as a human person equal to adults by dignity and rights (mainly since the second half of the 20th century). The idea of 'rights of the child' conquered global public opinion, has transformed the status of children in many legal systems, and continues to improve their lives in all continents.

The first UN Special Rapporteur on the Right to Education wrote (E/CN.4/2002/60)[82]:

> 30. The history of human rights can be depicted through two broadening concentric circles, the first showing a gradual extension of recognized rights and the second an incremental inclusion of those previously excluded. The rights first bestowed upon adult, propertied, white men have been gradually extended to women, then to non-white adults and later also to children.

1.2.1 Advent of the rights of the child

The rights of the child have been addressed by writings since the 19th century, at least, in the context of the progress of knowledge about childhood and the infantile medicine (the term 'paediatrics' dates back to the 1870s).

On 23 February 1923, the International Save the Children Union/*Union Internationale de Secours aux Enfants* approved the first Declaration of the Rights of the Child, in its 4th General Congress, in Geneva. The so-called "Geneva Declaration" had a brief preamble and five paragraphs. On 26 September 1924, it was unanimously endorsed by the League of Nations

(5th session), following a proposal from the Chilean Delegation, also in Geneva. Although the word 'right' only appears in the title, it was the first time that a Declaration of Rights was adopted by an Intergovernmental Organisation.

The greatest precursor of children's rights was Janusz Korczak (pseudonym of Henryk Goldszmit) – a Polish doctor, writer, educator, passionate about childhood and children. He was influenced by the New Education Movement, notably Pestalozzi, Froebel, Montessori, Decroly, Dewey, as well as Tolstoy. His orphanage in Warsaw was a small republic, with its constitution, parliament, tribunal and newspaper. When, on 6 August 1942, Nazi troops took its more than 190 children to the Treblinka extermination camp, Korczak entered the gas chamber with them.

On 20 November 1959, the UN General Assembly proclaimed a new Declaration of the Rights of the Child, with a Preamble and ten Principles. It was considered a revolutionary document, at the time. The idea of 'rights of the child' began to penetrate national legal systems, contributing to the 'democratisation' of Family Law, i.e. the recognition of the equal dignity and rights of all its members. The term 'paternal power' (*pater potestas*) was progressively replaced with 'parental authority' and then 'parental responsibility'.

The spirit of the 1959 Declaration was, however, still predominantly welfarist: the child was addressed more as *object of the Law* than as *subject of rights*.

1.2.2 Convention on the Rights of the Child

On 20 November 1989 – the day of the 30th anniversary of the 1959 Declaration – the UN General Assembly adopted a Convention on the Rights of the Child. According to its Article 1: "For the purposes of the present Convention, a child means every human being below the age of eighteen years unless, under the law applicable to the child, majority is attained earlier". It is a definition covering ages with different levels of development and needs, requiring a modulated application of the Convention.

The main features and content of the UN Convention are as follows:

- It is a treaty, i.e. a legally binding international instrument.

- It is the most comprehensive legal international instrument on the rights of the child, because:

    - it gathers together all the rights recognised to the child (which were dispersed in more than 80 international instruments, at the universal and regional levels, an abundance that was one of the arguments of the opponents to the need of a Convention);

    - it universalises rights that, until then, only had been recognised at the regional level or by jurisprudence (as the right of the child to be heard in legal or administrative cases concerning it);

    - it adds new rights (as the right to preserve his or her identity, the right to enjoy his or her own culture, the right to know his or her rights).

    - it enhances the level of protection by making compulsory rights that, until then, had been only a matter of recommendations (as the rights of handicapped children); by imposing new obligations to States (as to abolish traditional harmful practices, and to take measures in favour of children victims); by reinforcing the interdiction of discrimination;

- It is one of the most extensive treaties on human rights, recognising civil, cultural, economic and social rights (except the political rights whose exercise is subjected to a minimum age reserve).

- It was the most quickly adopted human rights treaty (about ten months after its adoption).

- It is the most universal human rights treaty, as it is in force in 196 States, including all UN Member States, except the US that only signed it.

- It is probably the most translated legal international instrument, after the 1948 Universal Declaration.

The Convention is composed of a Preamble, three Parts, and 54 Articles:

- The Preamble invokes general principles regarding human rights and children's rights.

- Part I (Articles 1-41) sets out the rights of the child and the corresponding obligations of States Parties.

- Part II (Articles 42-45) contains provisions on the enforcement of the Convention, in particular the establishment of a Committee on the Rights of the Child.

- Part III (Articles 46-54) consists of final provisions.

The Convention substantial norms (Part I) include two groups of rights:

- general human rights, i.e. recognised to every human being (except political rights);

- specific rights of the child required:

    - by the importance of preserving the family ties, as the right not to be separated from his or her parents without a very strong reason, and to maintain personal relations with both father and mother, in the case of separation;

    - by the children' immaturity, vulnerability, dependence, needs of development, as well as their protection against all forms of negligence, violence and exploitation;

- by the special needs of the most vulnerable groups of children, including children with disability;

- by the psychological specificity of the childhood, such as the right to play and to other activities particular to these ages.

The rights of the child are sometimes summarised in three 'Ps': Protection, Provision, Participation – a synthesis subscribed by the Committee on the Rights of the Child. A fourth 'P' could be added: Prevention.

The Convention was reinforced by two Protocols in 2000:

- Optional Protocol to the Convention on the Rights of the Child on the sale of children, child prostitution and child pornography (entered into force on 18 January 2002)

- Optional Protocol to the Convention on the Rights of the Child on the involvement of children in armed conflict (entered into force on 12 February 2002)

A third Protocol was adopted in 2011 and entered into force on 14 April 2014:

- Optional Protocol to the Convention on the Rights of the Child on a Communications Procedure.

It should be noted that, as underlined by the Committee (CRC/GC/2003/5)[83], "the other international human rights instruments apply to all persons below the age of 18 years" (para. 23).

At regional level, an African Charter on the Rights and Welfare of the Child was adopted in 1990 by the Organisation of African Unity, and a European Convention on the Exercise of Children's Rights was adopted in 1996. There is also a Charter of the Rights of the Arab Child (League of Arab States, 1983) and a Covenant on the Rights of the Child in Islam (Organisation of Islamic Cooperation, 2005).

There are many other legal instruments on the rights of the child at the universal and regional levels.

At the national level, the influence of the UN Convention has also been impressive. Numerous countries changed their laws and even their Constitutions.

1.2.3 Protection of the rights of the child

Parents are *naturally* the first responsible for the rights of their children, as the Convention recognises (mainly in Articles 5 and 18). However, *legally and politically,* the main party responsible for all rights of all persons are States, as we know. The most general framework of the obligations of States Parties to the Convention is laid down in Articles 2.1, 3.2 and 4.

Like other human rights core treaties, the Convention established, as already said, a Committee to supervise its implementation. States Parties to the Convention undertake to report to it periodically on the measures taken, the progress made and the obstacles encountered. It is also empowered by the Third Protocol to receive complaints ("communications") alleging violations of children's rights.

At the regional level, the African Charter on the Rights and Welfare of the Child (1990) established an African Committee of Experts on the Rights and Welfare of the Child. The European Convention on the Exercise of Children's Rights (1996) also established a Standing Committee. There is an Islamic Committee too.

At the national level, when the Convention was adopted, there were national institutions devoted to the rights of the child in only three countries (Norway, Costa Rica and New Zealand). At present, there are dozens, with varying names: Children's Ombudsman, Children's Rights Commissioner, *Défenseur des Enfants, Defensor de los Derechos del Niño,* etc.

The promotion and protection of the rights of the child is the *cause* of thousands of NGOs, at the international and national levels.

In 1954, the UN General Assembly recommended that, "with effect from 1956, a Universal Children's Day shall be instituted by all countries [...] observed on the date and in the way which each considers appropriate" (Resolution 836 (IX), 14 December)[84]. National days vary from country to country but, within the UN framework, the Universal Day is celebrated on 20 November, the date of the proclamation of the 1959 Declaration and adoption of the 1989 Convention.

The International Community took two great initiatives concerning children:

- In 1990, a World Summit for Children, meeting in the UN Headquarters, New York, on 29-30 September, adopted unanimously a World Declaration on the Survival, Protection and Development of Children and a Plan of Action for Implementing the World Declaration on the Survival, Protection, and Development of Children in the 1990s.

- In 2002, a Special Session on Children of the UN General Assembly, meeting from 8 to 10 May to balance the implementation of the 1990 Plan of Action, adopted a new Declaration and Plan of Action for "A World Fit for Children".

Here is the seriousness of what is at stake: The rights of children and the rights of adults are in a circular relation analogous to the Möbius Ring – the protection of the rights of children begins with the protection of the rights of adults, which begins with the protection of the rights of children. The violations of human rights chain themselves in a vicious circle of reproduction of poverty, ignorance, suffering, exclusion, violence, between generations, through children, who suffer from the violation of the rights of adults, especially from the misfortune of their parents.

1.2.4 Ethics of the Rights of the Child

The Committee on the Rights of the Child highlighted (CRC/GC/2001/1)[83]: "Children's rights are not detached or isolated values devoid of context but exist within a broader ethical framework which is partly described in Article 29 (1) and in the Preamble to the Convention." (para. 7) It is an ethical framework illuminated by "the core value of the Convention: the human dignity innate in every child and his or her equal and inalienable rights" (para. 1).

The rights of the child carry an ethical significance – a reflection of the Ethics of Human Rights – fundamentally because they outlaw the discrimination of children on account of their age and command their special protection by virtue of their age. They recognise and protect both the ethical-legal equality and the bio-psychological difference of children, i.e. the fullness of their dignity and rights, as human beings, while taking into account their immaturity, vulnerability and perfectibility, as children.

The Ethics of the Rights of the Child may be summarised into the following Principles:

- *Primacy of the "best interests of the child"*
- *Love, respect, and responsibility for the child*
- *Evolving autonomy of the child*
- *Priority of children*

These Principles are far-reaching in the everyday life of children – in the family, in school, in society. It follows a brief justification.

1.2.4.1 Primacy of "the best interests of the child"

The notion of "child's interests" emerged in the French Civil Code promulgated by Napoleon in 1804. During the 19th century, it expanded as a principle of self-limitation of adults' power over children, in particular within the family. The "special protection" of children has become a principle of Childhood Law, inspiring the legislation on nurseries and child labour, for example.

The principle of the primacy of the "best interests of the child" entered International Law with the 1959 Declaration of the Rights of the Child (Principle 2). Thereafter, it was endorsed by several international instruments, in variable formulations, such as the Convention on the Elimination of All Forms of Discrimination against Women (United Nations, 1979). The 1989 Convention consecrated it as a principle-guide for the exercise of public and private responsibilities concerning children (Article 3.1)[86]:

> 1. In all actions concerning children, whether undertaken by public or private social welfare institutions, courts of law, administrative authorities or legislative bodies, the best interests of the child shall be a primary consideration.

This principle is recognised by several Constitutions, as well as in number of Acts concerning children and their rights.

There is a significant international and national jurisprudence on the primacy of the best interests of the child.

Being a principle, the best interests of the child are not legally determined. Nor could they be, because, in addition to be a principle, general by nature, they have a meta-juridical content, i.e. they cannot be defined only by Law, abstractly, but must be established with the contribution of other knowledge, in each case and context. Their interpretation was addressed by the Committee on the Rights of the Child in its General Comment 14 (2013) "on the right of the child to have his or her best interests taken as a primary consideration (Art. 3, para. 1)" (CRC/C/GC/14)[87]. According to the Committee, this principle displays a large amplitude, to include all actions and omissions which, directly or indirectly, may affect children, individually or collectively. So understood, practically all policies affect children in one way or another.

Being a principle-interface between the ethical universality and the cultural particularity of the rights of the child, his or her best interests may be flexibly approached, as long as they are not *familiarised* or *nationalised*, to serve as a Trojan Horse of cultural relativism and other interests incompatible with respect for the dignity and rights of the child. No cultural particularities justify disregard for the best interests of the child.

Recognising the child in the fullness of his or her legal personality, the Convention on the Rights of the Child is like an *ethical lighthouse* that should illuminate and guide adults in their search and respect for child's best interests, which should be the most general principle for interpreting its gaps and obscurities, as well as for resolving possible conflicts of rights.

Summing up: Interpreted within the framework of the 1989 Convention, the best interests of the child are superior to cultural, national, family and other interests not compatible with the respect for his or her dignity and rights, may be superior also to the child's immediate interests, and are not different from the best interests of a democratic society and of humankind in becoming.

1.2.4.2 Love, respect and responsibility for the child

Love is perhaps the most powerful human sentiment – a universal and perennial theme in the history of literature and arts. The desire to be loved is the most profound expression of the most profound need of a human being: to be recognised. Its satisfaction, in infancy, is the primary source of a lifetime's feelings of love[88]...

Love is a theme also frequent in the history of childhood and education. Loving children is not, however, as *natural* a feeling as it is generally deemed.

Is there a 'right to love'?

Human rights are the juridical expression of a feeling of love for our common humanity, underlying the millennial principle of the Golden Rule, reflected in the Gospel message "Love one another".

The 1959 Declaration and the 1989 Convention are not unaware of the value of affectivity for the well-being and development of the child. The Declaration[89] affirms: "The child, for the full and harmonious development of his personality, needs love and understanding. He shall, wherever possible, grow up in the care and under the responsibility of his parents, and, in any case, in an atmosphere of affection and of moral and material security." (Principle 6) The Convention[90] reaffirms: "Recognising that the child, for the full and harmonious development of his or her personality, should grow up in a family environment, in an atmosphere of happiness, love and understanding" (Preamble, para. 6).

However, the formal recognition of a 'right to love' would exceed the power of Law and would not guarantee a feeling of love. The transformation of a need into a right, the passage from morality to legality, imply the determination of the corresponding obligations, with the possibility of recourse in case of non-compliance. But in the realm of sentiments there are no obligations or guarantees. Only in grammar may the *imperative* to love be pronounced. That is why 'love' is a term so unusual in International Human Rights Law.

Love for a child is a *sentiment* but should be first and foremost a *sentiment of responsibility*. It is, first of all, of course, a sentiment of biological attachment or of compassion towards a human being so fragile, vulnerable, dependent, seductive. However, in the era of the rights of the child, it should be principally a *sentiment of responsibility for his or her human rights*.

Children are entitled to the responsibility of adults, especially their parents, both because of their fragility and their dignity and perfectibility. A responsibility to be exercised as wise and serene dialectic of love-authority, in the best interests of the child (see 2.3.1).

In sum: There is not, nor can there be, a right to love, but a child has *right to the love of his or her rights*. In this sense, the entire Convention on the Rights of the Child is an oath of love.

1.2.4.3 Evolving autonomy of the child

During the drafting of the Convention, in the context of the debate raised by participation rights, the inclusion of a general clause on the "evolving capacities of the child" was suggested, which would eventually be worded in Article 5. Its position in the Convention's structure is significant of the role assigned to it as a provision balancing the rights of the child and "the responsibilities, rights and duties of parents" or other persons responsible for the child, which should be respected by State. Therefore, "the responsibilities" precede (because they are the justification of) both the "rights" and the "duties":

- to give the child "in a manner consistent with [his or her] evolving capacities", that is, taking into account both his or her immaturity and development,

- "appropriate direction and guidance in the exercise by the child of the rights recognised in the present Convention" (thus, without impositions).

This idea is also mentioned in Articles 12.1 and 14.2 and is connected with other provisions. Article 12.1 indicates as criterion "the age and maturity of the child" that is an objective (age) and a subjective (maturity) one.

Domestic legislation is variable concerning minimum age for the exercise of this or that right. What practically matters most is finding the right balance between child's protection and autonomy.

Therefore, the legitimacy of parents' intervention derives (descending) from the (descending) inability of children to exercise their rights autonomously.

1.2.4.4 Priority of children

The priority of children is, in a way, an extension of the primacy of the best interests of the child. It is an imperative of the vulnerability and potentiality of childhood, proclaimed before and after the 1989 Convention, whose Article 3.1 uses the singular "child" and the plural "children". These individual and collective dimensions were highlighted by the Committee on the Rights of the Child in its General Comment 7 (CRC/C/GC/2005/7/Rev.1),[91] where it refers to the "Best interests of individual children" and the "Best interests of young children as a group or constituency" (para. 13).

The Declaration on the Survival, Protection and Development of Children, approved by the World Summit for Children, on 30 September 1990[92], closed by stating: "There can be no task nobler than giving every child a better future." (para. 25) In order to achieve this, the Plan of Action for Implementing the Declaration stressed that it commanded "the principle of a 'first call for children' – a principle that the essential needs of children should be given high priority in the allocation of resources, in bad times as well as in good times, at national and international as well as at family levels" (para. 33). And justified:

> 3. Progress for children should be a key goal of overall national development. […] As their individual development and social contribution will shape the future of the world, investment in children's health, nutrition and education is the foundation for national development. […]
>
> …
>
> 36. … There is no cause which merits a higher priority than the protection and development of children, on whom the survival, stability and advancement of all nations – and, indeed, of human civilization – depends.

1.2.5 International Law of the Child

Children's Law has been traditionally a Minors' Law, as a subdomain of Family Law, whose pillars are the filiation and the paternal power (*patria potestas*).

The drafting of the Convention on the Rights of the Child was crossed by the tension between two approaches: *protection-approach* (as "childhood is entitled to special care and assistance") and *rights approach* (of the child as human rights holder). A *child-centred approach* prevailed, giving rise to a new International Law of the Child that deals with children's human rights internationally recognised and protected, at the universal and regional levels. Its radical novelty consists in the movement from the traditional (naturalist) vision of the *child-object of Law* towards a new (ethical) vision of the *child-subject of rights,* which (s)he should be allowed to exercise with increasing autonomy, as his or her capacities develop, with the concomitant modulation of the intervention of adults, namely mothers and fathers.

The core of the new International Law of the Child lies in the rights and freedoms recognised in Articles 12 to 17 of the 1989 Convention: the right to express his/her own views in all matters affecting the child, duly taking into account her/his age and maturity (Article 12); the right to freedom of expression (Article 13); the right to freedom of thought, conscience and religion (Article 14); the right to freedom of association and peaceful assembly (Article 15); the right to privacy (Article 16); the right of access to information (Article 17).

These are the cornerstones of the new International Law of the Child:

- Fullness of the legal personality of the child as a human being equal to adults by dignity and rights.

- Primacy of the best interests of the child as general principle of interpretation, application and expansion of his or her rights.

- Evolving capacities of the child to exercise his or her human rights autonomously or assisted by adults, if necessary.

1.2.6 Revolution of the Rights of the Child

The Convention on the Rights of the Child represents a historical deepening of the ideal and logic of human rights, culminating an evolution that truly means a revolution, as it is generally recognised by both its advocates and its detractors. It is a visionary text.

The Revolution of the Rights of the Child is fully identified in these words of the Committee on the Rights of the Child (CRC/C/GC/8, 2 March 2007)[93]: "The Convention asserts the status of the child as an individual person and holder of human rights. The child is not a possession of parents, nor of the State, nor simply an object of concern." (para. 47)[94] It amounts to an ethical and juridical revolution, but is, above all, the beginning of a deeper cultural one, long lasting, because it must transform mentalities and customs.

For this reason, the Revolution of the Rights of the Child encounters strong resistance, illustrated by certain reservations made by States Parties to the UN Convention, which are incompatible with International Law when they claim the primacy of domestic Law, or safeguard traditional cultural practices incompatible with respect for the child's human rights, or have a too general scope.

A surprising example of resistance is the position of the US, a State that, although having already signed the Convention (1995), still not ratified it, despite having played an important role in its *travaux préparatoires* (as well as in the creation of the United Nations and the legislative history of the 1948 Universal Declaration). The most powerful resistance comes from religious lobbies sustaining a fundamentalist mindset about family rights. The apocalyptic arguments of the opponents to the ratification of the Convention are not shared by eminent jurists and numerous American NGOs.

Underlying much of the cultural, sociological, psychological, resistance against the recognition of rights to children is a misunderstanding: to recognise rights to children is to take them away from parents. The rights of children are not rights against their parents, who have no rights over the human rights of their children. If they are respected, children become adults who are more developed, conscious, creative, happy, responsible. And better citizens and educators of their children.

The 'Bastille' of the Revolution of the Rights of the Child, is the right to education.

1.3 Right to education

1.3.1 Rising…

Three eras may be roughly distinguished, at least in the Western world, before the recognition of education as human right:

- Education as mostly a familial matter – the longest era.
- Education as a national interest – from some centuries ago.
- Education as international concern – from the late 19th century.

Education has always been regarded as a *(natural) right of the Family,* based on procreation and generally supported (and shared) by religions.

The school was appearing, in various cultures, as a more or less elitist institution dedicated to instruction. In the Western world, over centuries, only the Catholic Church was able to assure formal education that was practically a privilege of its clergy. From the Renaissance, by the advent of the modern Nation-State, education has also progressively become a Public Interest and a *(political) right of the State.*

Comenius and Rousseau were perhaps the major precursors of the right to education, for these main reasons: Comenius 'preached' the universality of education as imperative of the essential human educability, Rousseau questioned the legitimacy of the educational power, alongside with that of the political power.

Education is a word absent from the French Declaration of the Rights of Man and the Citizen (1789), as well as from the precedent American Bills of Rights, but the ascending phase of the French Revolution (1789-1793) was driven by the utopia of a *new man* and a *new people,* fueled by the belief in the indefinite human perfectibility and in the omnipotence of an education of reason (by Enlightenment, in a transfigured school) and of heart (by learning Republican virtues through civic feasts, in particular).

During the 19th century and the first half of the 20th century, instruction and the principle of compulsory schooling progressively entered the Constitutions. However, this did not necessarily entail the recognition of a right.

When was a true "right to education" recognised, for the first time?

At the beginning of the *travaux préparatoires* (drafting) of the Universal Declaration of Human Rights, in 1947, a documentary volume prepared by the UN Human Rights Division (*Documented Outline/Project Annotated,* 2 June 1947) (E/CN.4/AC.1/3/Add.1)[95] included 55 constitutional texts and other documents containing provisions on human rights. Almost all included provisions relating to education and school, but only the Soviet and the Cuban Constitutions used the expression "right to education", which was also found in three draft International Bills of Rights (American Law Institute, American Federation of Labour, Inter-American Juridical Committee). That is why we read sometimes that it is in the Soviet Constitution of 1936 (Article 121) that one finds, for the first time, the explicit recognition of a right to education. Yet already the Brazilian Constitution of 1934 (Article 149)[96] stated:

> Education is the right of everyone and must be provided by the family and by the Public Authorities, which must provide it to Brazilians and foreigners domiciled in the country, in such a way that it enables efficient factors of the moral and economic life of the Nation, and develops in the Brazilian spirit the awareness of human solidarity.

At the international level, education was first recognised as a right on the American continent: In 1948, the Charter of the Organisation of American States, which includes several references to education, devotes its Article 49 to the right to education, and the American Declaration of the Rights and Duties of Man consecrated to it its Article XII.

Some months later, education has been proclaimed, for the first time at the universal level, as an *(ethical) human right,* in Article 26 of the Universal Declaration of Human Rights.

Consequently, although in the history of great ideas there is a time when it is no longer night, but day is not yet fully born, talking about the recognition of the "right to education", before the 20th century, sounds anachronistic. Indeed, *right to education*:

- is not just a (*natural*) *right* of children, morally opposable to parents;

- is not only a (*social*) *right,* increasingly vital for the economic development and political life of a nation, justifying compulsory schooling;

- is now, above all, a (*individual*) *right,* internationally recognised and protected as a *human right* essential for the flourishing of beings endowed with aptitude for rationality, morality, creativity and responsibility.

1.3.2 International Education Law

International Education Law is a relatively recent branch of the leafy tree of International Human Rights Law. It may also be narrowly or broadly defined:

- Narrowly defined, the scope of International Education Law covers the legal dimensions of the human right to education: sources, normative content, mechanisms of protection, case law, doctrine.

- Broadly defined, International Education Law should not overlook an introduction to the human rights and to the rights of the child as a necessary general framework within which the international profile of the right to education can be outlined and its specificity understood, as well as answered questions the approach to education as a human right may raise; and should include the study of its origins in the history of education and human rights, as well as a conceptualisation of the legal, political, and pedagogical (theoretical and practical) implications of its normative content.

- **Sources**

International Human Rights Law is composed of varied instruments, as we know: their scope may be universal or regional, their legal force may be conventional or declaratory, their content may be general, specific or categorical. The main universal normative framework of International Education Law is as follows (see Appendix 1):

- Universal Declaration of Human Rights
  (United Nations, 1948, Article 26)

- International Covenant on Economic, Social and Cultural Rights
  (United Nations, 1966, Articles 13 and 14)

- Convention on the Rights of the Child
  (United Nations, 1989, Articles 28 and 29)

- Convention against Discrimination in Education
  (UNESCO, 1960)

At the regional level – Council of Europe, Organisation of American States (OAS), Organisation of African Unity (OAU, African Union since 2002) – there are the following principal legal instruments with provisions on the right to education:

- *European region*

  - First Protocol to the European Convention on Human Rights
    (1952, Article 2)

  - European Social Charter
    (1961, revised in 1996, Article 17 and others)

- European Charter on Education for Democratic Citizenship and Human Rights Education
  (2010)

  Still on the European continent, there are the Charter of Fundamental Rights of the European Union (2000, Article 14 and Article 32) and the Commonwealth of Independent States Convention on Human Rights and Fundamental Freedoms (1995, Articles 27 and 28).

- *American region*

- Charter of the Organisation of American States
  (1948, Article 49 and others)

- American Declaration of the Rights and Duties of Man
  (1948, Articles XII and XXXI)

- Additional Protocol to the American Convention on Human Rights in the Area of Economic, Social and Cultural Rights (Protocol of San Salvador)
  (1988, Article 13 and others)

- Inter-American Democratic Charter
  (2001, Articles 16 and 27)

- Social Charter of the Americas
  (2012, Article 19 and 23)

- *African region*

- African Charter on Human and Peoples' Rights
  (Banjul Charter)
  (1981, Articles 17 and 25)

- African Charter on the Rights and Welfare of the Child
  (1990, Articles 11, 14, 16 and 20)

- Protocol to the African Charter on Human and Peoples' Rights on the Rights of Women in Africa
  (2003, Article 12 and others)

- African Youth Charter
  (2006, Article 13 and others)

Legal instruments including provisions on the right to education were adopted in other regions by the following Organisations:

- Arab Charter on the Rights of the Child
  (League of Arab States, 1983, available in Arabic only)

- Cairo Declaration on Human Rights in Islam
  (Organisation of Islamic Cooperation, 1990)

- Arab Charter on Human Rights
  (League of Arab States, 2004)

- Social Charter
  (South Asian Association for Regional Cooperation (SAARC), 2004)

- Covenant on the Rights of the Child in Islam
  (Organisation of Islamic Cooperation, 2005)

- Human Rights Declaration
  (Association of Southeast Asian Nations (ASEAN), 2012)

There are provisions concerning education in other branches of International Law, notably International Labour Law, International Health Law, International Environmental Law, International Refugee Law, International Humanitarian Law and even in International Criminal Law (attacking and destroying educational facilities, depriving education on ethnic grounds, using education to incite genocide).

There are provisions on education/right to education in more than one hundred treaties and other international legal texts[97].

In accordance with the titles of the 1966 International Covenants, there are five categories of human rights: civil, political, economic, social and cultural rights. As the right to education is concerned, the Committee on Economic, Social and Cultural Rights said in its General Comment 11 (E/C.12/1999/4)[98]:

> 2. … It has been variously classified as an economic right, a social right and a cultural right. It is all of these. It is also, in many ways, a civil right and a political right, since it is central to the full and effective realization of those rights as well. In this respect, the right to education epitomizes the indivisibility and interdependence of all human rights.

- **Definitions and terminology**

The moral and functional integration of children into the groups and cultures where they are born is a need and a concern as old as human communities.

There are plentiful definitions of education in the history of the pedagogic thought, varying from broader to narrower conceptions.

- The educational phenomenon, broadly considered, includes all experiences and influences, intentional and unintentional, which contribute to forming the personality of each human being.

- Education, narrowly defined, is an intentional, organised process of communication and learning, by the new generations, the values, knowledge, competencies (abilities, skills), sentiments, attitudes, behaviour, through which human communities ensure their survival, reproduce their identity and each of their new members form their personality.

At the beginning of the drafting of the Universal Declaration Article 26, le French term *droit à l'instruction* (right to instruction) was used. It was René Cassin (French Delegate) who proposed, during the third session of the Commission on Human Rights (Lake Success, 1948), the replacement of the word *instruction* with *éducation*, that is a broader concept.

Eleanor Roosevelt (American Delegate and President of the Commission) proposed, in the Drafting Committee of the Declaration, the replacement of the term "primary" education with "elementary" education, which was accepted, but "primary" has prevailed in subsequent main instruments. Another amendment proposed by Roosevelt was the replacement of the words "for children" with "everyone", in order to include adults. In the Commission, the UNESCO representative (Pierre Lebar) and the China Delegate (Peng Chun Chang) proposed to add the term "fundamental", having in view courses for adults who have not been able to attend or complete elementary schooling. The proposal was approved. In the UN General Assembly Third Committee, the drafting Subcommittee proposed to replace the term "elementary education" with "fundamental education", but the two terms (elementary and fundamental) were kept.

Since the 1970s, the term "basic education" (*éducation de base* in French), has come into general use, but there is no international agreement on its scope:

- it may be synonymous with elementary/primary education/school;
- it may have a component of pre-school education and/or secondary school;
- it may cover the entire school education, except higher education;
- it may include the education of adults.

In general, basic education means the component of a school system that should be free and compulsory. Secondary education is a zone with variable geometry, between primary/basic and tertiary education. The Education 2030 Framework for Action[99] refers to "basic education (that is, pre-primary, primary and lower secondary education) for all" (para. 6).

1.3.3 Normative content of the right to education

As we know, the constituent elements of the structure and normative content of a right are its entitlement (right-holders), object (specific value) and exigibility (duty-bearers). What follows is a brief presentation of the normative content of the right to education in accordance with International Education Law.

1.3.3.1 Right-holders

Like every human right, the right to education is a right of "everyone": children and adults, women and men, whatever their differences, belongings, particularities and circumstances. Three priorities are justified, however:

- Priority of children, given the intensity of their educability, the resonance of education in their destiny and the life of societies, and because it is in the dawn of life that a whole life may be won or lost.

- Priority of girls, because of their enduring discrimination and of the repercussion of mothers' education on the family planning, health, well-being and development of children, as well on society at large.

- Priority of illiterate adults, who are hindered in their ability for being and living humanly, with repercussions on the education of children and in the social development.

Some more vulnerable groups of children discriminated against, often left behind, deserve special attention and protection too. They include: children with disability, children affected by HIV/AIDS, LGBTQI children, pregnant girls, working children, street children, children living in remote rural areas, orphaned children, children institutionalised, children hospitalised, imprisoned children, children affected by armed conflicts, internally displaced children, indigenous children and children belonging to minorities (ethnic, linguistic, religious and other), migrant children (nomadic, immigrant, refugee, asylum-seeker), children with learning difficulties, etc.

As a child is dependent on his or her parents, and because every human being lives in communities, families and States are co-holders of the right to education. However, their rights are not own and competing rights, but functional and complementary, assigned to fulfil their responsibilities.

The right to education bears a particular collective dimension when it comes to more culturally vulnerable communities, such as indigenous peoples, and also a general collective dimension, as a legitimate Public Interest.

In this context, it should be stressed that, while the purpose of education carries both individual and social dimensions, and although learning to know, to respect and to appreciate the wealth of cultural heritages and identities of the human communities should be a permanent concern of education, cultural beliefs, values and traditions should not impair the subjective ethical core of the right to education, which shall never be undermined by collective interests.

1.3.3.2 Object

The educational phenomenon consists in learning. The aptitude to learn amounts to the *mother* of the plurality of intelligences developed by learnings accomplished by each and every one, lifelong, according to their needs, possibilities, interests. There are as many intelligences as differences of intelligence.

The right to education fundamentally means right to learn. Therefore, determining its object amounts to answering the following main interrogations: Learning … for what? … what? … how? …

The object of the right to education comprehends thus its purpose and mediations. The purpose (aims) consists in the values and principles which should inspire and guide education. The mediations include persons and institutions, learnings and methods, the materials and the cultural and social environment. The principal international provisions on the right to education (see Appendix 1) command its purpose, describe the structure of a public education system and recognise educational liberties.

- *Purpose*

Education is purposeful, by definition. Nevertheless, the inclusion of the aims of education in Article 13.1 of the International Covenant on Economic, Social and Cultural Rights gave rise to some controversy during its *travaux préparatoires*, especially at the 8th session of the Human Rights Commission (E/CN.4/SR.285, 23 May 1952)[100]. Over time, the aims of education have been legally enhanced and densified, being now strong established:

- In the 1948 Universal Declaration, they are laid down in Article 26 second paragraph.

- In the 1966 International Covenant, they are laid down and improved in Article 13 first paragraph, immediately after the right to education entitlement.

- In the 1989 Convention, they are expanded in an autonomous Article (29.1).

According to the present International Education Law, the purpose of the right to education may be summarised as follows:

- Development of the human personality – freely, fully, harmoniously – and of the sense of the personal worth, dignity and uniqueness.

- Internalisation of the Ethics of Human Rights, as Ethics of the Humanity, and of other cultural values compatible with its respect.

- Preparing for an autonomous and responsible life – as human being, citizen, worker, parent – in a democratic society and a globalised world.

The purpose of the right to education is therefore inextricably individual and social, moral and instrumental, national and international.

- *Public system of education*

Family continues to be paramount for children's care and education, but school has become the principal institutional mediation of education in contemporary societies, a place where children and young people spend most of their days. A public education system, with a free and compulsory component, is the main obligation of each State regarding the right to education.

According to the International Standard Classification of Education (ISCED 2011)[101], a complete school system includes the following levels:

Level 0 – Early childhood education
Level 1 – Primary education
Level 2 – Lower secondary education
Level 3 – Upper secondary education
Level 4 – Post-secondary non-tertiary education
Level 5 – Short-cycle tertiary education
Level 6 – Bachelor's or equivalent level
Level 7 – Master's or equivalent level
Level 8 – Doctoral or equivalent level

- *Liberties of education*

Liberties recognised by International Education Law are the liberties of families with regard to the education of their children and the liberty to establish and direct educational institutions[102]. They must respect the aims prescribed by international standards as well as minimum national standards. There is also the academic freedom, not formally included in the object of the right to education, but implicit in it.

It should not be lost of sight, however, that the main liberty in education is the liberty of the subject of the right to education (see 2.2.2).

- *What school learnings?*

The main international provisions on the right to education do not spell out the learnings basic school education should ensure, but there are indications in other important texts and documents. Among them, the following ones are highlighted: A General Comment, three documents approved by major international meetings, and three UNESCO Reports.

o General Comment

It is the first General Comment of the Committee on the Rights of the Child.

o Three documents approved by major international meetings:

- World Declaration on Education for All: Meeting Basic Learning Needs
(Jomtien, Thailand, 1990)

- Dakar Framework for Action – Education for All: Meeting Our Collective Commitments
(Dakar, Senegal, 2000)

- Incheon Declaration
(Incheon, Republic of Korea, 2015)

o Three UNESCO Reports

- *Learning to be – The world of education today and tomorrow*
(International Commission chaired by Edgar Faure, 1972)

- *Learning: The treasure within*
(International Commission chaired by Jacques Delors, 1996)

- *Reimagining our futures together: A new social contract for education*
(International Commission chaired by HE Sahle-Work Zewde, 2021

Another UNESCO Report deserves to be mentioned: *Rethinking education: towards a global common good?*, authored by a Senior Experts' Group in the context of the preparation of the Incheon World Education Forum.

According to these documents, the right to education should guarantee learnings necessary to realise the primary purpose of the right to education: the development of the various dimensions of the human personality – physical, emotional, aesthetic, ethical, intellectual, professional, family, civic, international. They are summed up in the often quoted *four pillars* identified by the Delors Report[103] in the "Pointers and recommendations" of its Chapter 4: "Education throughout life is based on four pillars: learning to know, learning to do, learning to live together and learning to be."

Accordingly, a sound basic school education should include common and optional learnings:

- *Common learnings*
  - *Learning tools*

    Alphabetical literacy (reading, writing), mathematical literacy, digital literacy, plurilingualism.

  - *Fundamental learnings*

    Universal values, humanist and scientific knowledge necessary to an enlightened and compassionate worldview, as well as functional competencies (abilities, skills) essential for the existence's quality, especially for critical thinking, creative problem-solving, communication, relation and collaborative work, as well as for rational and reasonable decision-making.

- *Optional learnings*

  Individually chosen learnings meeting the diversity of talents and interests, including vocational preparation, for the sake both of everyone self-fulfillment and the advancement of the society at large.

The mediations of the right to education also include, as above noted, persons and methods, which will be addressed elsewhere.

1.3.3.3 Duty-bearers

The exigibility of human rights concerns, as we know, persons or entities to which they are opposable, i.e. with responsibilities and obligations for their satisfaction.

The responsibility for the education of children is firstly incumbent on their parents or legal substitutes, supported and supervised by State. Their responsibilities, as well as the corresponding rights, are affirmed in many international legal instruments. Family is a unique place in children's lives, because it all begins... in the beginning. It should be valued and treated as the most deeply touching influence on the life and destiny of a human being, with resonances throughout society.

However, the satisfaction of the whole object of children's right to education exceeds families' means. States hold the principal responsibility – legally and politically – for the implementation of all rights for all.

International Community carries a subsidiary responsibility regarding human rights, as already said. The Convention on the Rights of the Child, for instance, mentions "international co-operation in matters relating to education" (Article 28.3)[104]. In the opinion of the Committee on Economic, Social and Cultural Rights (General Comment 11, E/C.12/1999/4, 10 May 1999)[105], "the international community has a clear obligation to assist" (para. 9).

The promotion and protection of human rights is a general obligation, as we know.

The right to education is self-opposable too, i.e. a duty of each one towards him/herself. It is a right-duty, more than any other human right, because at stake is the *humanisation* itself (see 1.3.9). Is there a more transcendent individual duty than the duty to accomplish the personal perfectibility or educability as fully as possible?

As States are the main responsible for the right to education, their obligations are being highlighted.

1.3.4 States' specific obligations

We know what the general human rights obligations of States are (see 1.1.4).

Regarding the right to education, the Committee on the Economic, Social and Cultural Rights devoted to Article 13 of the respective Covenant its General Comment 13 (E/C.12/1999/10)[106], which describes its normative content (para. 4-42), points out States' obligations (para. 43-57), gives examples of violations (para. 58-59) and addresses obligations of other international actors (para. 60). Three categories of obligations are distinguished: "General legal obligations" (para. 43-48), "Specific legal obligations" (para. 49-56) and a "minimum core obligation" (para. 57).

As general legal obligations are concerned, the Committee recalls: "The right to education, like all human rights, imposes three types or levels of obligations on States Parties: the obligations to respect, protect and fulfil. In turn, the obligation to fulfil incorporates both an obligation to facilitate and an obligation to provide." (para. 46) For instance: *to respect* includes respecting the liberty of parents and private education establishments; *to protect* includes protecting children against possible abuses of parents' or private actors' liberty; *to fulfil* includes supporting disadvantaged groups by means of financial and other appropriate egalitarian measures.

The general legal obligations common to economic, social and cultural rights, in particular, are described in Article 2 of the Covenant, to which the Committee devoted its General Comment 3 (E/1991/23)[107]. It begins by stating (italics added):

> 1. Article 2 is of particular importance to a full understanding of the Covenant and must be seen as having a dynamic relationship with all of the other provisions of the Covenant. It describes the nature of the general legal obligations undertaken by States Parties to the Covenant. Those obligations include both what may be termed (following the work of the International Law Commission) *obligations of conduct* and *obligations of result.*

With regard to the right to education: *obligation of conduct* is, for example, to adopt an action plan to eliminate illiteracy; *obligation of result* is, for example, to achieve a certain rate of pre-school attendance.

Some obligations are "of immediate effect", as the Committee notes in General Comment 13, exemplifying (italics added):

> 43. While the Covenant provides for progressive realization and acknowledges the constraints due to the limits of available resources, it also imposes on States Parties various obligations which are *of immediate effect*. States Parties have *immediate obligations* in relation to the right to education, such as the "*guarantee*" that the right "will be exercised *without discrimination* of any kind" (Art.2.2) and the obligation "*to take steps*" (Art. 2.1) towards the full realization of Article 13. Such steps must be "deliberate, concrete and targeted" towards the full realization of the right to education.

The Committee recalls that, in General Comment 3, it had reaffirmed that States Parties have "a minimum core obligation to ensure the fulfilment of at least minimum essential levels" of each entitlement, including "the most basic forms of education" (para. 57).

As the "Specific legal obligations" are concerned, one may distinguish three levels, corresponding to the three aforementioned 'layers' of the normative content of human rights: minimum obligation/content, full obligation/content and expanded obligation/content.

The minimum obligation/content of the right to education comprises five elements, in the Committee's view:

- respect for the principle of non-discrimination;
- conformity of education with the purpose of the right to education;
- guarantee of free and compulsory elementary/primary or basic education;
- adoption of a national strategy accounting for the entire public education system;
- respect for the liberties of education that meet international and national standards.

Concerning the full obligation/content, the Committee, endorsing and expanding the '4-A scheme' proposed by the first Special Rapporteur on the Right to Education in its Preliminary Report (E/ CN.4/1999/49, para. 50)[108], considered that "education in all its forms and at all levels shall exhibit the following interrelated and essential features" (para. 6), namely: availability, accessibility, acceptability, adaptability. This scheme has become canonical, but it can be improved.

Indeed, if 'availability' and 'accessibility' are more quantitative, 'acceptability' and 'adaptability' are mainly qualitative in nature.

Acceptability of education refers especially to its contents and methods. The contents should meet the values and principles of the right to education international provisions, as well as national minimum educational standards. The methods should exclude everything not compatible with the respect for the dignity and rights of the subjects of the right to education and encourage their participation in learning, in school life and social life in general. Adaptability of education means that learnings should be relevant, i.e. respond to the individual needs, aptitudes and interests, as well as to collective needs, and have the flexibility allowing them to meet particular circumstances, to be up to the advancement of knowledge and technologies, and to adapt to unpredictable situations.

So understood, "acceptability" and "adaptability" may be largely subsumed into the concept of quality of education, which has a better recognised and stronger normative identity.

Quality should not be dissociated from equality as an ethical-legal principle whose *raison d'être* is the reality of diversity. Equality and diversity are both protected by the principle of non-discrimination.

Indeed, diversity may reflect a lack of equality or be an expression of liberty. In the first case, it calls for a policy of equity, through measures of "positive discrimination", with a view to inclusion. Goal 4 of the 2030 Agenda for Sustainable Development (United Nations, 2015) reads: "Ensure inclusive and equitable quality education and promote lifelong learning opportunities for all." (see Appendix 2)

Therefore, the full obligation/content of States relating to the right to education could be categorised in this way:

- *Availability*
- *Accessibility*
- *Quality*
- *Equity*

These categories of obligations are briefly described next.

1.3.4.1 Availability

Availability means the existence of a public education system with the necessary resources (human, material, financial). Schools are needed in sufficient number, which are safe, healthy, decent, functional learning environments, minimally comfortable, desirably beautiful, with clean drinking water, gender-sensitive sanitation, electricity if possible, convenient playgrounds. The school equipment should include, as far as possible, refectory, library, computers, sport facilities, etc. Class sizes should be acceptable and the teaching-learning materials should be free from ethnic prejudices or gender stereotypes. Teachers with the necessary qualities, qualifications, status and motivation are required.

1.3.4.2 *Accessibility*

Accessibility includes the following main dimensions: legal, economic, geographic, architectural, linguistic.

- *Legal accessibility*

  Legal accessibility means the recognition of the right to attend school, without any discrimination, in particular for categories of more vulnerable children. One aspect of legal accessibility is administrative accessibility, i.e. not being conditioned by undue or unachievable requirements, such as certificates of birth. However, there may be no discrimination *de jure* (legal), active, but remaining *de facto* (real), passive discrimination, in public policies, in the practice of schools and the behaviour of teachers.

- *Economic accessibility*

  Economic accessibility means, not only the absence of direct costs to attend basic schooling, but also the inexistence of 'hidden fees' and indirect costs in general, which may be an obstacle to its attendance, such as transport, school uniforms, study materials or other. Access to higher levels of schooling should not be hindered by lack of resources and must be progressively free. Affordability implies the possibility of support and may justify other measures in favour of groups traditionally discriminated against.

- *Geographical accessibility*

  Geographical accessibility means that the distance between the place of residence and the school is not excessive or dangerous and that there is transport or even accommodation for children who live too far away from the school. Accessibility may also be ensured under the form of distance learning, using appropriate technological means.

- o *Physical accessibility*

  Physical accessibility means, in particular, that school facilities are prepared to receive children with mobility limitations.

- o *Linguistic accessibility*

  Linguistic accessibility means that the language used, especially in pre-school and primary school, is not a barrier to learning (see 2.3.4).

1.3.4.3 *Quality*

Just as the centre of gravity of classical Political Philosophy is traditionally the question of the "good regime", the major theories in the history of education are conceptions of a "good education". The famous 'Second Bill of Rights'[109] proposed by US President Franklin Roosevelt in his message to Congress on the State of the Union, on 11 January 1944, included "The right to a good education". *Good education* is what is now meant as "quality education".

Quality education has become a slogan since the late 1980s. One may distinguish two main approaches to education quality:

- *Human capital approach*

  This approach reflects the neoliberal ideology, whose 'commandments' are profit, market freedom, competition, deregulation and privatisation of the economy, public disinvestment, minimal State. As education is concerned, neoliberalism advocates its liberalisation and privatisation, with politico-ideological and economic-financial arguments, including the following: freedom of choice, competition for improving education quality, reduction of public expenditure.

- *Human right approach*

  This approach is inspired by the normative integrity of the right to education, reflecting human rights values and principles. As wrote the first Special Rapporteur on the Right to Education in her Preliminary Report (E/CN.4/1999/49)[110]:

> 13. ... Human rights law specifies the purpose and objective of education, increasingly calling for the mainstreaming of human rights throughout the contents and process of education. From the human rights viewpoint, education is thus an end in itself rather than merely a means for achieving other ends. Some economists may, however, define education as efficient production of human capital and classify all its human rights dimensions as externalities. *A definition of people as human capital obviously differs from defining people as subjects of rights* [italics added].

However, there is no precise and consensual definition of quality in education. The main international reference is the first General Comment of the Committee on the Rights of the Child (CRC/GC/2001/1)[111] that reads (italics added):

> 2. Article 29 (1) not only adds to the right to education recognized in Article 28 a qualitative dimension which reflects the rights and inherent dignity of the child; it also insists upon the need for education to be *child-centred, child-friendly and empowering,* and it highlights the need for educational processes to be based upon the very principles it enunciates. [...]
>
> ...
>
> 9. ... while Article 28 focuses upon the obligations of States Parties in relation to the establishment of educational systems and in ensuring access thereto, Article 29 (1) underlines *the individual and subjective right to a specific quality of education.* Consistent with the Convention's emphasis on the importance of acting in the best interests of the child, this Article emphasizes the message of child-centred education: that *the key goal of education is the development of the individual child's personality, talents and abilities,* in recognition of the fact that *every child has unique characteristics, interests, abilities, and learning needs. [...]*

Consequently, more than the mere right of access to whatever education available, the right to education is the right to a well determined education quality. The overarching criterion of quality eduction should be *consistent with the radically personal purpose of the right to education, as a human right,* because what *matters* most, politically and pedagogically, is the human magnitude of the personality education can generate.

In addition to this paramount personal dimension, the quality of education has a necessary social dimension, obviously, requiring contextually relevant, variable contents, appropriate to communities circumstances and needs. This implies, notably, to balance the establishment of a national curricular framework, consistent with the normative integrity of the right to education, with devolving reasonable autonomy to schools, provided that teachers are professionally able to assume it, that is, duly selected, prepared and strongly motivated.

The *UNESCO Education Strategy – 2014-2021* (Chapter 2 – Towards a new education agenda after 2015)[112] stated (italics added): "UNESCO advocates a *humanistic* and *holistic* vision of education as a fundamental human right that is essential to personal and socio-economic development." This is the vision of education quality inspiring the Incheon Declaration and the Agenda Education 2030 (see Appendix 2).

- *Humanistic* is an education anchored in the ethical core of the human right to education, i.e. an education unfailing committed with the cultivation of the highest human aptitudes, which are Rationality, Morality and Creativity, and the superior values of education, which should be Liberty, Reciprocity and Responsibility (see 2.2.2).

- *Holistic* is an education meeting the multiple dimensions of the human personality and existence – physical, emotional, aesthetic, ethical, intellectual, professional, family, civic, international – and not losing sight of the human rights interdependence, individually and collectively.

A humanistic and holistic education is necessarily *universalist*, that is, with perspectives and concerns without borders.

This is a vision of education quality absolutely opposed to an education captured and misused by ethnic reflexes, cultural traditions, religious beliefs, partisan indoctrination or neoliberal economism.

Quality education is, therefore, a complex concept. Its factors are multiple, interactive, complementary: material and non-material, tangible and intangible – from the location, architecture, decoration and equipment of schools to the values, principles, aims, programmes, methods, assessment criteria, manuals, qualifications of staff, school climate, without overlooking, upstream, the quality of family life as the *foyer* of individual destinies.

At the end of the day, the deepest sources of education quality are the quality of parents' love (see 2.3.1) and the personal qualities of education professionals (see 2.3.7).

1.3.4.4 Equity

Equity is a moral-juridical notion of Greco-Latin origin used by national and international Tribunals and Courts as a principle of moderation of the literal, formal rigour of the Law, animated by a sense of justice. As education is concerned, it is a principle of generalisation of its quality as human right, taking into account the human rights interdependence, i.e. the various conditions of possibility, effectiveness and usefulness of the right to education.

Indeed, children and adolescents are not abstract entities, 'pupils' without body and cradle, but sons and daughters of mothers and fathers who live within cultural, social and economic horizons involving their destinies. Their right to education is compromised if other rights and their educators' rights are not satisfied. For example, unhealthy or hungry children are diminished in their ability and willingness to learn; young educated and trained for a profession they have chosen, but have not the opportunity to exercise, suffer an unfair frustration and limitation of their horizons of life, with prejudice also for their communities and society at large; illiterate mothers and fathers or with little education, or unemployed, as well as education professionals undermined in their professionality and professionalism, are affected in their ability to be responsible for the right to education.

In the view of the Committee on Economic, Social and Cultural Rights (General Comment 11, E/C.12/1999/4)[113] (let us recall), "the right to education epitomizes the indivisibility and interdependence of all human rights" (para. 2).

In 2017, UNESCO published *A Guide for ensuring inclusion and equity in education*[114], following which: "The central message is simple: *every learner matters and matters equally*." (p. 12) In Ecuador, the *Ley Orgánica Reformatoria de la Ley Orgánica de Educación Intercultural* (Organic Law Reforming the Organic Law on Intercultural Education)[115] includes in Article 2, among numerous Principles, the following ones:

> *Equity*
>
> Equity guarantees access, permanence, learning, participation, promotion and completion in the Education System for all. It guarantees equal opportunities for communities, peoples, nationalities, priority groups, in vulnerable situations, through affirmative action measures, fostering an inclusive school culture, eradicating all forms of discrimination, generating policies and applying inclusive educational practices.
> ...
>
> *Inclusion*
>
> Inclusion recognizes the diversity of people, peoples and nationalities, individual and collective differences, as an opportunity for the enrichment of society, through active participation and interaction in family, social, educational, work dimensions, in general in all social, cultural and community processes; [...]

To sum up: Equity is a principle of inclusion of diversity and support of equality.

1.3.5 States' paramount obligations

1.3.5.1 Directing education towards the purpose of the right to education

This is one of the elements of the minimum obligation/content summarised above. The General Comment 13 of the Committee on

Economic, Social and Cultural Rights begins the description of the normative content of the right to education by stating:

> 4. States Parties agree that all education, whether public or private, formal or non-formal, shall be directed towards the aims and objectives identified in Article 13 (1). The Committee notes that these educational objectives reflect the fundamental purposes and principles of the United Nations as enshrined in Articles 1 and 2 of the Charter.

It reaffirmed: "States Parties are required to ensure that curricula, for all levels of the educational system, are directed to the objectives identified in Article 13 (1)" (para. 49) and others subsequently adopted, which "reflect a contemporary interpretation of Article 13 (1)" (para. 5). The liberties of education are recognised under condition that they "conform to the educational objectives set out in Article 13 (1) and certain minimum standards" (para. 29).

Therefore, school programs "inconsistent with the educational objectives set out in Article 13 (1)" are in breach with the right to education (para. 59).

1.3.5.2 Guaranteeing free compulsory basic education

This is another element of the aforementioned minimum obligation/ content. The Committee said in its General Comment 13:

> 51. As already observed, the obligations of States Parties in relation to primary, secondary, higher and fundamental education are not identical. Given the wording of Article 13 (2), States Parties are obliged to prioritize the introduction of compulsory, free primary education. This interpretation of Article 13 (2) is reinforced by the priority accorded to primary education in Article 14. The obligation to provide primary education for all is an immediate duty of all States Parties.

There is no normative instrument or programmatic text determining the duration of compulsory schooling, which is variable. The only existing formal consensus, in this respect, is that its starting age should be determined and the age of its term shall not be under the minimum age for access to employment, according to the ILO Convention concerning

Minimum Age for Admission to Employment (C138)[116], which provides: "The minimum age specified in pursuance of paragraph 1 of this Article shall not be less than the age of completion of compulsory schooling and, in any case, shall not be less than 15 years" (Article 2.3). Exceptions are admitted.

School obligation usually begins between 5 and 7 years of age and its duration has increased progressively, over the decades, depending upon economic development, with a tendency to absorb secondary schooling.

1.3.5.2 Regulating and supervising private education

This obligation is not included in the minimum obligation/content, but what is at stake is increasingly worrying (v. 3.9).

In General Comment 13, the Committee affirms that States Parties are "obliged to establish and maintain a transparent and effective system which monitors whether or not education is, in fact, directed to the educational objectives set out in Article 13 (1)" (para. 49), as well as to supervise compliance with "certain minimum standards", which "may relate to issues such as admission, curricula and the recognition of certificates. In their turn, these standards must be consistent with the educational objectives set out in Article 13 (1)." (para. 29)

The non-existence of "a transparent and effective system to monitor conformity with Article 13 (1)" is an example of violation of Article 13 of the Covenant (para. 59).

1.3.6 Protection and justiciability of the right to education

- **Protection**

The mechanisms of the UN human rights protection system apply to the right to education, of course, where appropriate. The UN Committees most directly concerned with the right to education are the Human Rights Committee, the Committee on Economic, Social and

Cultural Rights, the Committee on the Rights of the Child, the Committee on the Elimination of All Forms of Discrimination against Women and the Committee on the Rights of Persons with Disabilities. And there is the Special Rapporteur on the Right to Education[117].

Within UNESCO's specific framework, there are a constitutional mechanism, a procedure created by the Executive Board, and bodies established by two instruments.

- In accordance with its Constitution (Article VIII), all Member States of UNESCO are required to report periodically on the follow-up they give to the normative instruments adopted by the General Conference. The right of communication (submission of complaints) of States is implicit in the Rules of Procedure of the General Conference (Rule 10.d) and of the Executive Board (Rule 5.2).

- There was no procedure to deal with the increasingly numerous communications addressed to UNESCO by individuals or groups, alleging violations of rights within its competence. This possibility has been created by the Executive Board in 1978: it is the '104 Procedure', so named after the Decision 104 EX/3.3 which established it.

- Two legal instruments have their own mechanisms:

    - Conciliation and Good Offices Commission to be responsible for seeking a settlement of any disputes which may arise between States Parties to the Convention against Discrimination in Education (1962)

    - Joint ILO/UNESCO Committee of Experts on the Application of the Recommendations concerning Teaching Personnel (CEART): Recommendation Concerning the Status of Teachers (1966) and Recommendation Concerning the Status of Higher-Education Teaching Personnel (1997)

There are normative instruments relevant to the right to education within the International Labour Organisation (ILO) framework, which has mechanisms, old and effective, to supervise compliance with its standards, to which trade unions can have recourse.

At the regional level, there are three systems of human rights protection, as we know: European, American, African. Moreover, there are some mechanisms in the Asian region, and in the Arab and Muslim world.

Plentiful NGOs are dedicated to the right to education, among them the Right to Education Initiative[118].

- **Justiciability**

The most important international Case Law on the right to education – and on human rights in general – is that of the organs of the European Convention on Human Rights (the former European Commission of Human Rights and the European Court of Human Rights, now merged in a permanent Court). It is the most significant contribution of European Education Law to International Education Law. Its principles were established mainly in the following classical Cases:

- *Case "relating to certain aspects of the laws on the use of languages in education in Belgium"* (1968)
- *Case Kjeldsen, Busk Madsen and Pedersen* (1976)
- *Case Tyrer* (1978)
- *Case Campbell and Cosans* (1982)

There is also the European Committee of Social Rights to oversee the respect of the European Social Charter, which includes the right to education. The Committee is competent to receive collective complaints. Its Case Law is already significant.

Within the European Union, the founding treaties of the European Communities did not refer to education. However, the progress and needs of the European integration project compelled the increasing intervention in the field of education. The Court of Justice of the European Communities (now Court of Justice of the European Union) eventually recognised a Community right to education, based principally on Articles 118 and 128 of the European Economic Community Treaty, in the following main Cases:

- *Donato Casagrande* (1974)
- *Forcheri* (1983)
- *Gravier* (1985)
- *Barra and Balizot* (1988)

The Court's jurisprudence caused a turn in the Community status of education.

The jurisprudence of international and national Courts has contributed to the normative development of the right to education, sometimes performing a law-making function. For example, the Constitution of India[119] refers to education several times, but a right to education was not formally provided for. In 1993, by answering the question "Whether the Constitution of India guarantees a fundamental right to education to its citizens?", the Supreme Court of India said in *Unni Krishnan, J.P. And Ors. Etc. … vs State Of Andhra Pradesh And Ors. … on 4 February 1993 (1993 AIR 2178, 1993 SCR (1) 594)*[120]:

> 31. Right to education is not stated expressly as a fundamental right in Part Ill [of the Constitution]. This Court has, however, not followed the rule that unless a right is expressly stated as a fundamental right, it cannot be treated as one. Freedom of Press is not expressly mentioned in Part III, yet it has been read into and inferred from the freedom of speech and expression.

In the wake of this jurisprudence, the Constitution of India was amended in 2002, and an Article 21A was added, so worded: "The State shall provide free and compulsory education to all children of the age of six to fourteen years in such manner as the State may, by law, determine". A Right of Children to Free and Compulsory Education Act (RTE Act)[121] was passed in 2009, coming into effect in 2010.

Other contributions to the normative development of the right to education have come from the quasi-jurisprudence and General Comments or General Recommendations of the UN Committees, and from the doctrine developed by the first Special Rapporteur on the Right to Education, in particular, as well as from the already mentioned Limburg Principles (1986), Maastricht Guidelines (1997) and Maastricht Principles (2011).

1.3.7 Singularity of the right to education

Some features distinguish the right to education.

- *It is the most complex human right*

The complexity of the right to education is due to the plurality of entitlement claims and competing interests (of children, families, States, religions, etc.), as well as to the multidimensionality of its object, reflecting the plurality of its purpose.

- *It is the most empowering human right*

Human rights empower, by their very nature, but the right to education may be considered the most empowering one. The Committee on Economic, Social and Cultural Rights begins its General Comment 13 (E/C.12/1999/10)[122] affirming:

> 1. Education is both a human right in itself and an indispensable means of realizing other human rights. As an empowerment right, education is the primary vehicle by which economically and socially marginalized adults and children can lift themselves out of poverty and obtain the means to participate fully in their communities. [...] Increasingly, education is recognized as one of the best financial investments States can make. But the importance of education is not just practical: a well-educated, enlightened and active mind, able to wander freely and widely, is one of the joys and rewards of human existence.

- *It is the only human right with a formally free element*

Being universal, human rights should be universally guaranteed, but the right to education is the only one with a formally free element:

primary or basic education. The Incheon Declaration (2015) states (see Appendix 2):

> 6. Motivated by our significant achievements in expanding access to education over the last 15 years, we will ensure the provision of 12 years of free, publicly funded, equitable quality primary and secondary education, of which at least nine years are compulsory, leading to relevant learning outcomes. We also encourage the provision of at least one year of free and compulsory quality pre-primary education and that all children have access to quality early childhood development, care and education. [...]

- *It is the only human right with a compulsory component*

Primary education is compulsory, a term apparently not compatible with the idea of 'right', but, in principle, an element of obligation does not necessarily prejudice the right concerned (see 3.3) and, in the present case, it is intended primarily for families and States.

- *Its normative content is among the most internationally developed*

International Education Law has become one of the most developed branches of International Human Rights Law, after International Labour Law, which is much older.

- *Its normative content includes elements from all international legal sources*

As we know, the right to education has international sources of *hard law* nature (formally binding, such as treaties), but most are of *soft law* nature (not formally binding, such as declarations or recommendations). Its normative content includes elements that are non-derogable, others that have become Customary Law and some others deserving the status of General Principles of Law and even of *Jus Cogens*[123].

1.3.8 Priority of the right to education

The human primacy of education is an idea crossing the history of the pedagogic thought. Over the centuries, education has been blamed, often and paradoxically, as the cause of all evils and valued as their main remedy. The universal conscience of its primacy – especially of first education and of moral education – is reverberated in proverbs of the wisdom of peoples and has always had prominent spokespersons.

Three human rights whose relative priority is generally recognised are the right to life, the right to development, and the right to education. The right to education is of transcendent importance for *human* life and development. Its priority – that is relative because of the human rights interdependence – was repeatedly invoked during the *travaux préparatoires* of its major international provisions, is recognised by International Human Rights Law, has been reaffirmed by jurisprudence, and is underpinned by doctrine. As stressed the first Special Rapporteur on the Right to Education (E/CN.4/2004/45)[124]: "Children cannot wait to grow, hence their prioritized right to education in International Human Rights Law. The damage of denied education while they are growing up cannot be retroactively remedied." (para. 8)

The priority of the right to education has been rediscovered, in a way, by International Community during the last decade of the 20th century, conferring to it unprecedented visibility on the International Agenda, as witness conferences, declarations, action programmes and other texts and initiatives. The 2014 *My World – The United Nations Global Survey for a Better World – Celebrating 7 Million Voices*[125] reported that about 1 in 1,000 people on the planet, from 194 countries, were asked "What would make *your* life better?" and could pick 6 out of 16 suggested priorities: "The overwhelming majority of the respondents prioritize 'A good education'. This is the case across all age groups, genders, education levels and HDI [Human Development Index] rankings."

The right to education is said to be an *unlocking, enabling, multiplier right*, an *equalising force*. *Key* is a term often used, especially in UN documents, to mean the paramount value of education. Sometimes it is said to be *a key*, other times it is called *the key*. The right to education is the key to the engine of human development, understood in the fullness of its individual, collective, cultural, political, economic, ecological dimensions.

Summing up, the right to education is a priority right because:

- A human being is not born as the Greek goddess Athena, who came adult and finished out of the head of Zeus. It is the only animal having a real aptitude for, and a vital need of, education.

- Everything in the life of a child, in particular, has educational effects, influencing the development of his or her personality and especially the formation of her or his moral conscience.

- It is through education that we learn that we have rights, how to claim and enjoy them, and also to respect the rights of others so that we can live peacefully and in solidarity.

- Education is the most powerful resource in the fight against poverty, oppression, injustice, violence, as well as for the protection of the rights of all minorities and, in particular, of ethnic identities.

- The right to education is a source of autonomy and citizenship, national and planetary, of utopia and rebelliousness liberating peoples, of the genius inherent in the inexhaustible perfectibility of the human species.

The international priority accorded to the right to education means that education is no more envisaged as only a matter of domestic and instrumental interest, but also as an ethical and international concern. If the connection between education, survival, work and economy has been the most socially and individually valued – and remains the most visible – the right to education is principally the most *humanising* human right, as it is consubstantial with human dignity.

1.3.9 Right to education and human dignity

Human dignity is like the backbone of the ethical subject underlying all the differences and contingencies of the empirical subjects, conferring equal rights whose ultimate sense is the development of the human personality, without arbitrary and unjust limitations. To the extent that they are inherent in dignity and contribute to the development of personality, all human rights have an ethical dimension, but the right to education has an incomparable ethical radicality: the development of the human personality is its specific value/object.

On the basis of the proposed conceptualisation (see 1.1.6.1), we could say, resorting to an informatic metaphor, that human dignity is formed of a *hardware* consisting in the biological infrastructure of the perfectibility or educability of the species, genetically *programmed*, and a *software* consisting in the perfecting of each of its members, culturally *programmable*, through education.

Given the dual nature of human beings – biological and cultural – two levels of human dignity may be distinguished, as already suggested: absolute dignity and relative dignity.

- *Absolute dignity* is the dignity inherent in membership of the human species, which lies in its perfectibility. It is the *genetic dignity*, objective, common.

- *Relative dignity* is the dignity dependent on the learning that realises the perfectibility. It is the *cultural dignity*, intersubjective, variable.

The human dignity relativity may be clarified by another metaphor:

- Members of the human species are born with 'wings', but without education they become atrophied, paralysed. They possess the *genetic dignity* of belonging to the species, but without realising the virtualities of their perfectibility. The "wild children" are tragic historical 'experiences' of this condition.

- If they learn to fly only over their territory of birth, human beings learn just their particular *ethnic dignity*, which may not tolerate differences, as was the case with Nazism, whose ideology of Aryan superiority justified the *Vernichtung* (annihilation) of the *Untermenschen* (subhumans).

- When they learn to fly over all seas and continents, they learn the universality of the *ethical dignity*, whose common 'temple' is the *genetic dignity*, where they meet, recognise, exchange and enrich each other, with the diversity of faces, clothes and songs of their *ethnic dignity*.

Therefore, human dignity is a worth that is possessed and learnt. It is a double learning: general and specific.

- The perfectibility or educability qualifying the human dignity is ontologically accomplished through education.

- The conscience of the personal dignity and the recognition of others' dignity depend on the moral orientation of education.

The consubstantiality between life, human dignity, right to education and development of the personality has been stressed by the jurisprudence. Examples:

- The German Federal Constitutional Court said (*1 BvR 112/65*, 14 February 1973, para. 28)[126]: "The system of values of the fundamental rights is centred in the free development of human personality and its dignity within the social community (BVerfGE 6, 32 [41]; 7, 198 [205]."

- The Supreme Court of India said in *Miss Mohini Jain vs State Of Karnataka And Ors on 30 July 1992 (1992 AIR 1858, 1992 SCR (3) 658)*[127], concerning fees charged by private schools: "The right to education flows directly from right to life. The right to life under Article 21 and the dignity of an individual cannot be assured unless it is accompanied by the right to education." (1.07)

- The South African Constitutional Court said in *Ferreira v Levin NO and Others* (CCT 5/95, 6 December 1995)[128]:

> (49) Human dignity cannot be fully valued or respected unless individuals are able to develop their humanity, their "humanness", to the full extent of its potential. Each human being is uniquely talented. Part of the dignity of every human being is the fact and awareness of this uniqueness. An individual's human dignity cannot be fully respected or valued unless the individual is permitted to develop his or her unique talents optimally. Human dignity has little value without freedom; for without freedom personal development and fulfilment are not possible.

- The Supreme Court of Israel Sitting as the High Court of Justice said, in 2011, in *Abu Libdeh v. Minister of Education (HCJ5373/08)*[129] (italics added):

> 26. ... The crucial importance of education in the life of the individual and in the formulation of his human existence, the centrality of education in determining a person's way of life and quality of life and the significance of this factor for the realization of his human dignity, ostensibly intertwine the right to education in its basic meaning with the value of human dignity [...]. *It seems that the right to education forms part of the "hard core" of human dignity, without which the value of personal dignity is materially and severely compromised* [...].

In sum:

- There is no more seminal a right than the right to education for the humanisation of the human species' children.

- For being a *semiotic animal,* Man is a *pedagogic animal,* that is, with an inexhaustible aptitude and vital need to learn.

- *The right to education is the key to the human dignity of life, because we must learn to be human and to live humanly.*

In concluding

International Human Rights Law is rooted in the subversion triggered by the ethical-legal individualism of the ideal of *Droits de l'Homme* (Rights of Man), from which is born the *New Law* of the French Revolution.

The right to education proclaimed by the Universal Declaration of Human Rights is new and has evolved, reaching superior coherence in the Convention on the Rights of the Child. It was mainly an evolution of the recognition of their subjectivity. Let us see.

According to Article 26.3 of the 1948 Universal Declaration: "Parents have a prior right to choose the kind of education that shall be given to their children." This provision was intended to protect children from totalitarian indoctrination by States. Nevertheless, it was only at the Third Committee of the United Nations General Assembly, in November 1948, that its wording was approved, but only by 17 votes to 13 with 7 abstentions (A/C.3/SR.148)[130].

Article 13.3 of the International Covenant on Economic, Social and Cultural Rights (1966) restricted the scope of Article 26.3 of the Universal Declaration[131]. Now, States Parties "undertake to have respect for the liberty of parents and, when applicable, legal guardians, [...] to ensure the religious and moral education of their children in conformity with their own convictions". Therefore:

- the word "right" has been replaced by "liberty",
- the term "priority" is omitted
- and it is not a question of "to choose the kind of education that shall be given to their children", but only "to ensure the religious and moral education of their children in conformity with their own convictions".

The Convention on the Rights of the Child (1989) no longer contains a provision equivalent to Article 13.3 of the 1966 Covenant.

This normative evolution culminates, therefore, in the full recognition of the ethical-legal autonomy of the child, who is no longer envisaged as subordinated to the discretion of mother and father.

Consequently, the right to education is a *new right* because of its *subjectivity, normativity* and *exigibility* as a human right.

- *Subjectivity* means that the right to education is a *right of every human being*, absolutely, whatever their gender, age, belonging and other particularities and circumstances. Families and States are not 'owners' of children and their human rights.

- *Normativity* means that the right to education is *right to an education in accordance with its normative integrity*, internationally agreed. It is not merely a right-reflection of a family and societal 'right' to decide, with more or less discretion, what is "good education".

- *Exigibility* means that the right to education is *justiciable*, i.e. its violation is liable to judicial recourse. It is not merely a moral and social right, at the mercy of the goodwill and convenience of families and States, "for your good"...

The birth of the *human right to education* has opened up a new Chapter in the History of Education. The *travaux préparatoires* (drafting) of its major international provisions illustrate the process of creation of International Law. The motivations of the decisions and dissident opinions of its jurisprudence document the evolution and confrontation of pedagogical mindsets.

The normative, jurisprudential, doctrinal and programmatic developments of the right to education have given rise to an International Education Law. It is the highest source of the contemporary normativity of education, having inseminated national Education Laws.

The superiority of International Education Law – as well as of the International Human Rights Law and the International Law of the Child – derives from International Law, which is no one's imposition. Its authors and direct addressees are States that *oblige themselves*.

The foundation of the superior validity of International Law is the normative rationality – representative and argumentative – of the political and diplomatic mechanisms of its drafting and approval within the institutional framework of the International Community, following the rules governing international treaty-making by States, through their Delegates and frequently with the participation of personalities with a high moral and intellectual stature, and of international civil society.

As a consequence, Education Law – that is, national legal normativity relating to or applicable to education (flowing from various legal areas) – should reflect International Education Law in which the State is party. It should therefore be recognised and studied as a new legal and pedagogical discipline, source of the principles of legitimacy and quality of education as a human right and global public good.

Indeed, being a new right, the right to education is *right to a new education.*

Chapter 2
New Education

Education is traditionally a domestic preserve – family and national. The institutional status of *son* or *daughter* and *pupil* has meant a *capitis diminutio* (diminished legal status) and could serve as a kind of suspension clause for the respect of the dignity and rights of children in particular. Within this paradigm, the child is treated as the 'property' of parents (and the State), who are the *Erziehungsberechtichte* (holders of the right of education) – an expression used by the Weimar Constitution (Germany, 1919), replicated in other constitutional texts, but not found in International Human Rights Law.

As the first Special Rapporteur on the Right to Education pointed out, "the entry of human rights has changed Education Law, which traditionally treated children as the object of education, specifying [only] the rights of parents, teachers and the State" (E/ CN.4/2001/52, para. 76)[132].

2.1 Rightful Education

It was against the *paradigm of the right of education* that emerged, at the end of the 19th century, on the American and European continents, the New Education Movement – or New School, *École Active* (Active School), Progressive Education, *Reformpädagogik* (Reformist Pedagogy) – whose main source of inspiration was Rousseau. It was the most powerful wave of renewal (and a fascinating chapter) in the history of education. Thousands of educators and prominent personalities attended its major congresses on different continents. In the documents and speeches of its protagonists one finds references, direct or indirect, to human rights, the rights of the child and the right to education – to its values and principles. In this regard, it is of some historical interest to note that one of the speakers at one of the Movement's congresses (in

Cheltenham, 1936) was Peng Chun Chang, Professor at Nankai University, Tianjin (China), Confucian philosopher, writer and diplomat, who would be one of the aforementioned Big Five of the Human Rights Commission who drafted the Universal Declaration, as Delegate of Nationalist China.

The human right to education reflects and universalised the ideal that, during about two decades, between the two World Wars, gathered so many educators and other militants of the renewal of education.

Well, if "education is not exempt from the rule of law" – as wrote the first Special Rapporteur on the Right to Education (E/CN.4/2000/6, para. 27)[133] – then the right to education is right to a *human right approach* of education (*human-rights-based*) that, under the Rule of Law, may be qualified as Rightful Education.

Rightful Education is not a mere word game of pedagogical appropriation of the prestige and legitimising effects of the juridical-political expression "Rule of Law". It conveys a very precise meaning: Just as Rule of Law means, at present, a political regime founded on the principle of respect for human dignity and rights, Rightful Education means education consistent with the normative integrity of the right to education.

The normative integrity of the right to education may be systematised in Principles of *Ethics of the Right to Education* from which stem *Educational Rights*.

2.2 Ethics of the Right to Education

The right to education has an ethical content – inscribed in the Ethics of Human Rights and the Ethics of the Rights of the Child – essentially because it is a *right of the human being* and no longer a *right over human beings*.

The major theories of education, in general, are structured by a conceptual trilogy evident, or underlying, in its main definitions, namely: *Perfectibility, Perfection, Perfecting*. That is why the traditionally central question of the theorisation of education is that of its ideal or purpose. General Laws of Education generally begin by stating the overall purpose of the respective public education system and the goals of each of its cycles, to which the specific objectives of each curricular learning contribute.

The Committee on the Rights of the Child stated in its first General Comment (CRC/GC/2001/1)[134], with reference to General Comment 13 of the Committee on Economic, Social and Cultural Rights (italics added):

> 1. Article 29, paragraph 1, of the Convention on the Rights of the Child is of far-reaching importance. The aims of education that it sets out, which have been agreed to by all States Parties, promote, support and protect *the core value of the Convention: the human dignity innate in every child and his or her equal and inalienable rights. These aims, set out in the five subparagraphs of Article 29 (1), are all linked directly to the realization of the child's human dignity and rights,* taking into account the child's special developmental needs and diverse evolving capacities. [...]

The purpose of education is thus the ethical substance of the normative integrity of the right to education. As set out in its main international provisions, expanded by other instruments of International Education Law, it may be summed up in the following Principles of Ethics of the Right to Education:

- *Primacy of the best interests of the subject of the right to education*

  It is a principle reflecting the general primacy of the subject of human rights and generalising the primacy of the best interests of the child in education.

- *Development of the human personality: free, full, harmonious*

  It is a principle identifying the specific value/object of the right to education, which should be the sense of all learnings necessary for its realisation.

- *Education for human rights as Ethics of Humanity*

  It is a principle reaffirming the traditional primacy of moral education, with the amplitude of its present conception, as ethical, civic and international education.

These principles are briefly justified next.

2.2.1 Primacy of the best interests of the subject of the right to education

The Vienna Declaration and Programme of Action (1993)[135] has reaffirmed (Preamble):

> … that all human rights derive from the dignity and worth inherent in the human person, and that the human person is the central subject of human rights and fundamental freedoms, and consequently should be the principal beneficiary and should participate actively in the realization of these rights and freedoms,

The principle of the primacy of the best interests of the subject of the right to education – rooted in the very subjective nature of human rights – is widely recognised, internationally and nationally, both at the legislative level and by jurisprudence and doctrine. For example, the Committee on Economic, Social and Cultural Rights stated in its General Comment 13 (E/C.12/1999/10)[136]: "When considering the appropriate application of these 'interrelated and essential features', the best interests of the student shall be a primary consideration." (para. 7) The General Education Law of Uruguay (2008)[137] recalls in its Article 5 (On the subject of education): "The holders of the enjoyment and effective exercise of the right to education are the learners." And it dedicates Title V, with only one Article (120), to the following "Specific Principle of Interpretation and Integration of the Law":

> For the interpretation and integration of the present Law, the best interests of the learner shall be taken into account, which consists in the recognition and respect of the rights inherent to his or her quality as human person. Consequently, this principle may not be invoked to the detriment of such rights.

Therefore, in case of conflict between the interests of the subject of the right to education, first of all a child, and the interests of fathers or mothers, of State or other interests, values and traditions, the former must prevail.

The best interests of the subject of the right to education should be held as the supreme principle of International Education Law. And what interest could be higher than the development of the human personality?

2.2.2 Development of the human personality: free, full, harmonious

The German Basic Law (*Grundgesetz*)[138] was the first Constitution to recognise the development of personality as a right, in its Article 2.1: "Everyone shall have the right to free development of his or her personality insofar as he or she does not violate the rights of others or offend against the constitutional order or the moral law." In subsequent Constitutional Law, the development of personality is recognised as a right or principle. In other cases, it was the jurisprudence that has derived it from constitutional norms.

Just as human dignity is recognised, sometimes, as a right, but is generally regarded as the principle-source of all human rights, also should the development of the human personality, more than one right among others, be taken as a principle.

In accordance with the jurisprudence of the European Court of Human Rights and the Constitutional Court of Colombia, in particular, the essence of the right-principle of the development of the human personality lies in the autonomy and self-determination of every human being, that is, in his or her aptitude and freedom to choose the ends and the means that give meaning to their existence[139]. Autonomy, broadly understood, has not only psychological, moral, intellectual, civic dimensions, but includes the conditions of an independent existence, especially the capacity and possibility to meet the subsistence needs and others necessary for a dignified life. Self-determination implies notably the right to private life, provided that it respects the rights of others and other values of the Public Order[140].

The development of the human personality is most often associated with the right to education, of course, because it is its specific value/object. The idea that it should be the overarching purpose of education was consensual during the drafting of Article 26 of the Universal Declaration of Human Rights. Minor discrepancies in the description of the dimensions of the development of the human personality have been overcome with their subsumption in the term "full". It must also be "free" (Article 22), "free and full" (Article 29.1). According to the Declaration of the Rights of the Child (1959) and the Convention on the Rights of the Child (1989), it must be "full and harmonious" (Principle 6 and Preamble, respectively).

The Committee on the Rights of the Child ties up development, uniqueness and best interests of each child (CRC/ GC/2001/1)[141], as already partly quoted:

> 9. … Consistent with the Convention's emphasis on the importance of acting in the best interests of the child, this Article [29.1] emphasizes the message of child-centred education: that the key goal of education is the development of the individual child's personality, talents and abilities, in recognition of the fact that every child has unique characteristics, interests, abilities, and learning needs. Thus, the curriculum must be of direct relevance to the child's social, cultural, environmental and economic context and to his or her present and future needs and take full account of the child's evolving capacities; teaching methods should be tailored to the different needs of different children. Education must also be aimed at ensuring that essential life skills are learnt by every child and that no child leaves school without being equipped to face the challenges that he or she can expect to be confronted with in life. […]
>
> …
>
> 12.… Education should be child-friendly, inspiring and motivating the individual child. Schools should foster a humane atmosphere and allow children to develop according to their evolving capacities.

The development of the human personality is today recognised as the highest aim of the right to education, both in International Education Law and in numerous Constitutions and General Laws of Education worldwide, as well as at the jurisprudential level, with special reference to the exceptional jurisprudence of the Constitutional Court of Colombia.

The legal principle of the free, full and harmonious development of the human personality enshrines the ideal proclaimed by the great authors of the history of pedagogic thought. It is the ideal of liberty, which implies reciprocity and responsibility. Learning liberty, reciprocity and responsibility should be considered the most fundamental learnings for the humanisation of the human species' children.

- **Liberty**

Liberty or freedom should be the central value of education, for the following main reasons:

- it lies at the ethical core of human dignity;
- it is the principle of legitimacy of the value of authority;
- it is the psychological and methodological condition of every true learning.

Human liberty is not *liberty-anomie* (without rules), nor *liberty-heteronomy* (subordinated), but *liberty-autonomy* (self-determining).

Liberty-autonomy is the superior form of human liberty.

- **Reciprocity**

There is no human liberty without reciprocity, i.e. the recognition of equal dignity and liberty of others. It is a principle underlying the Golden Rule and the Ethics of Human Rights as Ethics of Recognition.

Reciprocity is the most humanising dimension of the development of the personality.

- **Responsibility**

Liberty and reciprocity imply responsibility. Nowadays, there is a renewed ethical demand centred on personal responsibility. The imperative of responsibility extends to all fields of human action. There is talk of Ethics of Responsibility.

Responsibility is a major requirement of the morality of existence.

As a consequence, Liberty, Reciprocity and Responsibility should be prized as the superior values of education. They are the highest expressions of a humanely developed personality – flowers and fruits whose colours, odours and flavours are the Promised Land of our infinite humanisation... Their cultivation lies at the core of the *pedagogical responsibility*. The main responsibility of parents and education professionals is to help children, adolescents and young, with words and attitudes of affectionate serenity, learn thinking, acting and reacting rationally and ethically.

2.2.3 Education for human rights as Ethics of Humanity

The distinction of the human species lies, according to the proposed theorisation, in its perfectibility, which means educability or the ability and necessity of perfecting its members through the cultivation of the higher aptitudes or faculties contained in the human genome: rationality, morality, creativity. Human perfecting tends to be identified with moral perfecting, so that 'human' and 'educated' have a morally positive connotation.

- *Human* denotes belonging to humankind, but when we say "to treat humanely" we mean to act according to values and sentiments of respect, empathy and compassion for others. If someone seriously violates certain values, they are said to be "monsters".

- *Educated* is every human being who is born and grows up in a community, but when we say that someone is "an educated person", we mean *well-educated,* i.e. who behaves according to shared moral values. Not that (s)he has a high intellectual quotient.

Man can then be also defined as a *moral animal,* in the Kantian sense. But human beings are not born good or bad, compassionate or cruel. They learn to be so.

The conscience of the human primacy of morality profoundly influenced the drafting of the founding texts of the new international legal order after World War II, in particular Article 26 of the Universal Declaration of Human Rights, as well as the Constitutive Act of UNESCO[142], whose Preamble begins with the famous proclamation:

> The Governments of the States Parties to this Constitution on behalf of their peoples declare:
> That since wars begin in the minds of men, it is in the minds of men that the defences of peace must be constructed;

Indeed, Law can *write* rules in codes, but only education can *engrave* values in hearts.

The primacy of moral education should be, therefore, imperative and consist of learning the values, ideas, sentiments, attitudes, behaviours that most elevate above the animal condition. Learning, first and foremost, to put oneself in the shoes of others, in order to strive to understand them, and to act accordingly. It is the sense of the Golden Rule – the oldest and most universal moral principle, precursor of the higher values the species has invented for being and living better, condensed in Article 1 of the Universal Declaration: "All human beings are born free and equal in dignity and rights. They are endowed with reason and conscience and should act towards one another in a spirit of brotherhood."

- **Origins and evolution of education for human rights**

The 1948 Universal Declaration was proclaimed "as a common standard of achievement for all peoples and all nations", especially "by teaching and education" (last paragraph of the Preamble), and one of the aims of education should be "the strengthening of respect for human rights and fundamental freedoms" (Article 26.2).

Immediately after its proclamation, the UN General Assembly approved a Resolution on the "Publicity to be given to the Universal Declaration of Human Rights" (A/RES/217(III)D)[143], recommending to Member States its dissemination through every means, "principally in schools and other educational institutions". UN specialised agencies and NGOs were also invited to do so. To this effect, the Secretary-General was requested to make the Declaration available in the greatest possible number of languages (they are more than 550, at present)[144].

In 1950, the General Assembly approved a Resolution on a "Human Rights Day" (A/RES/423(V)), to be celebrated on 10 December 1948 of each year, the day of the proclamation of the Universal Declaration of Human Rights.

Over the decades, the normative and programmatic action of the United Nations, especially UNESCO, and other Intergovernmental Organisations, in the field of education for human rights, has become the most developed chapter of International Education Law. Here are some culminating moments and documents of its evolution:

- In 1974, UNESCO adopted the Recommendation on Education for International Understanding and Co-operation and Peace and Education relating to Human Rights and Fundamental Freedoms that continues to be the main international legal instrument in this field (it is about to be revised).

- In 1993, the Vienna Declaration and Programme of Action approved by the World Conference on Human Rights – that mentions education 28 times – devoted its Section II-D (para. 78-82) to "Human rights education".

- In 1994, the UN General Assembly proclaimed, "the ten-year period beginning on 1 January 1995 the United Nations Decade for Human Rights Education" (A/RES/49/184).

- In 1995, UNESCO adopted a Declaration and an Integrated Framework of Action on Education for Peace, Human Rights and Democracy, approved by the 44th Session of the International Conference on Education that took place in 1994, the year of the 20th anniversary of the 1974 Recommendation.

- In 2004, on the Human Rights Day, devoted to human rights education, the UN General Assembly proclaimed "the World Programme for Human Rights Education, structured in consecutive phases, scheduled to begin on 1 January 2005, in order to advance the implementation of human rights education programmes in all sectors" (Resolution 59/113). The fourth phase is ongoing (2020-2024), and the next one is being prepared.

- In 2011, was adopted a United Nations Declaration on Human Rights Education and Training (A/RES/66/137) that updates the definition of "human rights education" first given in the Plan of Action of the Decade for Human Rights Education launched in 1994 and developed by the 2005 World Programme for Human Rights Education.

- In the European continent, a Council of Europe Charter on Education for Democratic Citizenship and Human Rights Education was adopted in 2010. An umbrella-concept, common to the Council of Europe and the European Union, has been "European dimension of education"[145].

- **Broad content**

UNESCO Executive Board adopted, in 2016, "Draft guidelines for the preparation of reports by Member States on the application of the Recommendation Concerning Education for International Understanding, Co-operation and Peace and Education Relating to

Human Rights and Fundamental Freedoms" (199 EX/14 Part III, Annex)[146]. They read:

> 3. The 1974 Recommendation is applicable to formal, non-formal and informal education and to all levels, from pre-primary to higher and adult education and life-long learning. It concerns areas such as civics and ethics education, education for international understanding, solidarity and cooperation and/or other related subjects, such as peace education, human rights education or other areas of study that focus or include the teaching and learning of the above principles. Over time, these areas have evolved to include other topics related to education on sustainable development, climate change, global citizenship, preventing violent extremism, or others, which are also closely related to the original principles of the 1974 Recommendation.

The scope of education for human rights has, therefore, evolved, and its content has ramified, diversified, expanded. Its present broad, holistic content may be described as an ethical, civic and international education.

- It is an ethical education aimed at knowing and internalising the Ethics of Human Rights as Ethics of Humanity that may be summarised in the abovementioned rights-principles.

- It is a civic education, as human rights are the most fundamental rights of citizens, in a Rule of Law, with refractions in all places and dimensions of daily citizenship, making various learnings necessary.

- It is an international education, as the respect of human dignity and rights is leaven of justice and constitutes the foundation of peace, as stated by the founding texts of the contemporary international legal order.

Texts adopted by the International Community recommend with growing insistence the inclusion of education for human rights in family and school education, as well as in other education and training institutions and places, at all ages, especially for professions more exposed to possible disregard of human rights, such as the military, judges, lawyers, law enforcement officers, physicians, education professionals, social workers, etc.

Education for human rights is *about, through, and for human rights,* that is, for knowing, living, exercising, recognising and respecting human rights. It consists of values, knowledge, sentiments, competencies, attitudes, behaviours, i.e. has ethical, cognitive, emotional, praxeological dimensions. It should be experiential, transdisciplinary, but also requires specific learning. While each subject matter of education for human rights has its own history and thematic specificity, human rights are the substratum common to them. There are many guidelines drawn up by Intergovernmental and Non-governmental Organisations, for their organisation and methodology at all ages.

A Pedagogy of Education for Human Rights is a conception of its necessity, aims, contents, methodology (principles, activities, resources) and organisation.

- **A crucial right**

Education for human rights is a right – an element of the object of the right to education (Article 26.2 of the Universal Declaration). The Convention on the Rights of the Child contains this unprecedented provision in conventional Law (Article 42)[147]: "States Parties undertake to make the principles and provisions of the Convention widely known, by appropriate and active means, to adults and children alike." The United Nations Declaration on Human Rights Education and Training (2011)[148] begins by proclaiming (Article 1.1): "Everyone has the right to know, seek and receive information about all human rights and fundamental freedoms and should have access to human rights education and training." The sexennial Report on progress achieved in the implementation of the 1974 Recommendation during the period 1986-1991 (26 C/32 7, October 1991)[149] affirmed that, "apart from the international legal validity of human rights, they may be considered as the basis for a universal ethic to be known and conformed to by everyone who receives a formal education" (para. 46).

To learn the rights and responsibilities of being human and citizen in a country and the world is no less important than to learn reading, writing, mathematics or informatics. It is a matter of learning universal values and principles of good and evil, right and wrong, the desirable and the undesirable, giving sense to the individual life (and death), and necessary to pacify human and international relations.

Education for human rights as Ethics of Humanity lies at the heart of quality education. The scientific and technological progress are fabulous creations of the human genius that are increasingly enhancing our wellbeing and longevity, but how many unspeakable evils can they cause, if applied without the highest moral conscience? The powers the human species has conquered over nature and itself are already so great that their misuse may violate its very essence and threaten its survival.

In the era of Globalisation and of so many threats for the present and future, a vital and irreplaceable mission of school is conveying to the new generations fundamental values for the protection and reproduction of the ethical identity and unity of the human species, while respecting and valuing the legitimate and splendorous diversity of its members and creations.

In sum: Education for human rights as Ethics of Humanity is an element of the right to education crucial for every human being, all societies and the whole humankind, because:

- Education for human rights means a kind of implantation of the *symbolic prosthesis* of the species' superior *humanness*.

- It is in their values and sentiments that lives the *soul* of human beings and cultures and lies the possible *immortality* of the species …

Every human being can learn to *imprint* into the world his or her love for Humanity.

2.3 Educational Rights

The right to education is a normative complex of Educational Rights, stemmed from the Ethics of the Right to Education. Broadly understood, they are rights derived from the formal content of the object of the right to education or implicit in it or required by the human rights interdependence. They are foremostly the rights of children and adolescents within the two main institutions of education, family and school. They may be summed up as follows:

- Right to pedagogical responsibility
- Right to be different
- Right to respect for human dignity and rights in education
- Right to learn the and in the mother tongue
- Right to the comprehensiveness of the right to education
- Right to a rightful school
- Right to admirable education professionals
- Right of access to Internet
- Right to an effective remedy

These rights are more or less briefly justified next.

2.3.1 Right to pedagogical responsibility

The first right of the subject of the right to education, as a child, is the right to the responsibility of adults, primarily of mother and father. Responsibility for children's protection, of course, but also for the love and authority they need.

There is not a 'right to love', as we know. However, insofar as the educational relation has an axial affective dimension, especially in childhood education, there is a *pedagogical right to a pedagogical love*.

Parents' love is unique but may be problematic. They are generally deemed to want the best for their children, but what is best for children may not be what parents deem to be so. They love them in the way they know, they can, they need … When children are treated as biological 'property', it is a possessive love that may be repressive or permissive:

- *Repressive love* is a symptom of immaturity of adults in need of exercising power over *minors* to feel themselves *majors*, or a feeling reflecting religious or other convictions legitimising the 'appropriation' of children by parents.

- *Permissive love* is one motivated by psychological weakness or fear of 'losing' a son or daughter, making mothers and fathers 'hostages' of their whims and insolence, with educationally malignant effects.

Possessive feelings, with a repressive effect or for affective consumption, can result in a true *pedagogical infanticide.*

Whenever parents try to moor their children by means of repression or permissiveness, it may happen that they break the moorings and go out, do not come back, and sink… The sole legitimate and secure moorings are those of affection responsibly liberating. The alternative to authoritarianism is not laxity without borders or horizons. An authoritarian educator does not educate, but neither does one who is not respected. If the principle of the legitimacy of education, as a human right, should not be the 'law of the strongest', it should not be the 'law of the weakest', either.

If parents do not assume the authority necessary to carry out their responsibility, they lose credibility and respectability. Then, there is a sole alternative: either continuing to increasingly become hostages of the child they did not know to help become autonomous; or to try to correct past mistakes and to control the child hostage to himself or herself, but at the expense of principles whose application, at the appropriate time, would have been preventive. Children may be punished for behaviours permitted by the irresponsibility of adults …

The main resource of authority, in education, should be words, from the very beginning. For that, it is necessary that educators know to say the right word, at the opportune moment, and respect their words. Otherwise, this induces a kind of psychological deafness which obliges to multiply and even to cry the words. And when adults get involved in Homeric discussions with children the scene is pathetic ...

The most ethical and rational communication is dialogue, given the essential human intersubjectivity inherent in the human beings' relational and communicational nature. Dialogue is all the more authentic when it respects and values the alterity and transcends reciprocity. It is also the most educational communication to the extent that it harmonises the value of liberty with the value of authority. Education should be dialogic for ethical, psychological, epistemological, methodological and political reasons.

However, words are not the last word... in education. Everything is significant for a child, in particular, nothing is indifferent to him or her in the behaviours of surrounding adults. It is the everyday attitudes of mothers and fathers, other educators and adults, that sow the values and principles of education.

In short:

A child has right to be treated as equal and different by adults who are equal, but different. (S)he has a vital need for adults' love that be an adult love. A love that be not a drive for property and arbitrariness, but passion for otherness and freedom.

Loving pedagogically children, adolescents and young is to give them the best we have and know; to desire that they have what we could not have, that they know what we could not know, that they are what we could not be; to allow them to drink the overflowing chalice of the liquor of their age; to let them go so that they return ... But they have the right to both the 'yes' and the 'no' necessary for their protection and learning of the liberty, reciprocity and responsibility, which imply the exercise of authority.

Summing up:

Pedagogical responsibility is the responsibility of educators for the right of children to education with its affective and normative dimensions, i.e. as a right both to pedagogical love and to pedagogical authority.

- Pedagogical is the *love* that knows the need children have of authority for the formation of their personality. It is *the most complex love.*

- Pedagogical is the *authority* that, not being arbitrary, is felt as an expression of love. Knowing how to exercise it is *the most difficult knowledge in education.*

2.3.2 Right to be different

After the right to the pedagogical responsibility of adults, as a child, the most important right of the subject of the right to education, as a human being, is the right to be different.

The right to be different has collective and individual dimensions, but the first one is the most legally recognised in International Human Rights Law. However, because human dignity may be captured by collective representations not compatible with the respect of human rights, its recognition is always accompanied by a clause safeguarding the primacy of the individual dimension and thus the absolute respect for human rights.

The individual differences are not chosen or chosen:

- Differences not chosen are principally the physical or mental handicaps, and many cultural ones.

- Differences chosen are those resulting from the free development of the aptitudes, interests and options of each one.

The right to be different implies the right to the identity formed by differences. They are twin rights.

The collective and individual dimensions of differences and identities are interwoven. The individual identity is configured by family, community and culture where one is born. Family, inscription in a lineage, is the *foyer* of its configuration.

The individual identity is multifaceted. Each human being is a bundle of identities, with physical and symbolic markers, objective and subjective, making the 'first impression'... They are mainly the following ones:

- *Biological identity* is the identity *possessed* by the human species' children. It has a common genetic content and a singular genealogic one.

- *Ethical identity* is the identity *recognised* to every human being, just for being human. It consists in the recognition of his or her dignity and rights.

- *Cultural identity* is the identity *learnt* within the culture where each one grows. It is simultaneously a spontaneous and compulsory learning.

- *Civic identity* is the identity *attributed* to each newborn by parents and the respective society. It is written on an identification document.

- *Psychological identity* is the identity *felt* as uniqueness, unity and continuity. It is a dynamic, evolving identity, variable with the ages of life and social positions.

Consequently, in addition to its civic dimension, the individual identity has an objective dimension (biological), an intersubjective dimension (ethical), a trans-subjective dimension (cultural) and a subjective dimension (psychological). Psychological identity is the crystallisation of the individual identity as a composition of multiple identities, resulting from a diachronic and dialectic construction of socialisation and autonomisation.

The already quoted Universal Declaration on the Human Genome and Human Rights (UNESCO, 1997)[150] affirms that the human dignity "makes it imperative not to reduce individuals to their genetic characteristics and to respect their uniqueness and diversity" (Article 2.b).

The right to education – as right to free, full and harmonious development of the human personality – lies at the heart of the right to be different and to the corresponding identity. It should include:

- the right of the child to the difference of his or her age, first and foremost, that is the right to enjoy the happiness and irresponsibility of childhood;

- the right of every subject of the right to education to respect for their differences not chosen and the differences they should be allowed to choose.

The first Special Rapporteur on the Right to Education commented in her last Report (E/CN.4/2004/45)[151], shortly before her untimely death:

> 54. … International Human Rights Law demands substitution of the previous requirement upon children to adapt themselves to whatever education was available by adapting education to the best interests of each child. In our imperfect world, the right of each child to be regarded – and respected – as different remains a distant dream.

In conclusion:

- Cultures are not isolated, homogeneous, static units, but dynamic and increasingly interacting complexes of beliefs, values, ways of living, whose legitimate and valuable diversity is Common Heritage of Humanity.

- A culture is a collective enduring cradle, a symbolic milk, music unforgettable, but should not be a frontier, a destiny, imposing an obligation of identification and making human beings hostages of the culture in which they are born.

- The inevitability of the infusion of a cultural identity, during childhood, should not prevent the progressive liberty to create an original personal identity, open to the universal treasure of the fabulous human diversity and creations.

- The educational right to be different is a crucial right for Humanity in becoming, because it is by means of education that it is reborn and can perfect itself, through their children, if they are not expropriated of their right to be different and better.

2.3.3 Right to respect for human dignity and rights in education

The right to be different is inseparable from the principle of equality by dignity and rights. Respect for the dignity and rights of children and adolescents, particularly at school, is at stake when disciplinary sanctions are decided and applied, but not only.

In education, as in social life in general, rules are needed whose non-observance justifies sanctions. They are legitimate to the extent that they do not harm the values they are supposed to protect and promote. School disciplinary sanctions should not disproportionately affect the right to education or violate other rights of students. For example, temporary suspension of school attendance is acceptable if its duration is not excessive and difficult to overcome, but the definitive expulsion of a student in compulsory schooling breaches the right to education if (s)he has not a reasonable possibility to attend another school. Examples of sanctions involving the violation of other rights include deprivations of rest time and recreation, and even of lunch. And, typically, the traditional corporal punishment (see 3.1).

All forms of disciplinary violence contribute to making schools fearful and even dangerous places, including taunting, humiliation, harassment, aggression, whose frequent targets are children from poor backgrounds and other more vulnerable, such as children with disability, and children from minority groups.

Moreover, children and young people have the right to really participate in adults' decisions concerning them, both at home and school. Other rights are the right to freedom of thought and expression, including the most original expressions of their personality not incompatible with respect for school institutional dignity, safety and well-functioning, and other values of the Public Order.

Disrespect for children's and young persons' dignity and rights at school is not only a potential cause of learning disaffection, underperformance, indiscipline, school dropout, early marriage, but also a factor of risk and disruptive behaviour, including tobacco, alcohol and drug consumption, aggressivity against peers and teachers, social delinquency, as well as vulnerability to various forms of exploitation, such as sexual abuse, prostitution, forced labour, enrolment in armed conflict, etc.

2.3.4 Right to learn the mother tongue, and in the mother tongue

The major international provisions on the right to education do not entail a linguistic element.

The right of members of ethnic minorities to learn their language and culture in their own institutions is recognised, but a general right to learn in the mother tongue, at least in the early years of school (and pre-school) education, if it is different from the official language or languages, when it is recognised, the wording is vague and flexible, leaving States a wide margin of decision (and omission).

There are two irrefutable arguments in favour of the right to learn in the mother tongue:

- Mother tongue is not a choice, it is an identity heritage.

- If a child does not understand the language of teaching, how can (s)he learn?

Anyway, the applicability of the principle of non-discrimination is indisputable.

Learning in the mother tongue, when it is not national language, is recognised as a factor of equal opportunities. In such a globalised world and multilingual societies, the right to education should include the right to learn the and in the mother tongue, to learn the or one of the national languages and to learn at least one international language.

2.3.5 Right to the comprehensiveness of the right to education

The object of the right to education includes its full and expanded content, as has been explained. The following are some observations on certain aspects of its comprehensiveness.

- *Pre-school education*

The main international provisions on the right to education do not formally include pre-school education. This is especially surprising regarding the Convention on the Rights of the Child, despite proposals made during its *travaux préparatoires*. Nevertheless, various international instruments and documents recognise, expressly or implicitly, that pre-school education should be part of States' obligations[152].

The value and resonance of childhood education are well established.

- *Vocational education*

Vocational education is an element of the object of the right to education that has gained relevance in contemporary societies. The Committee on Economic, Social and Cultural Rights considers it an integral part of all levels of school education. It must include "education and training", i.e. not be merely instrumental, economistic, without a humanistic and cultural perspective, but holistic, envisioning – as recommended by the relevant international texts – the whole existence of those learning a profession, as human beings and citizens.

It is important to stress that, although a solid basic school education should include some professional preparation, this one should not undermine the paramountcy of the integrity of the normative content of the right to education.

- *Higher education*

Higher education is an element of the object of the right to education, albeit with formally less strong obligations for States. Available higher education should be accessible to those who are willing and demonstrate the ability to attend it (regardless of their economic condition).

Accessibility may be conditioned (*numerus clausus*), but according to objective and appropriate criteria, which are not discriminatory and take into account knowledge and experience other than those certified by school diplomas.

Higher education is part of tertiary education that includes all post-secondary education, in universities, polytechnics, and other similar institutions. It has been the main target of neoliberalism in education. Some States have withdrawn from funding it, favouring private taking over. Others have implemented 'cost-sharing' policies, economically and socially selective. Now, a shift seems to be on the way, in the face of evidence of the economic return of the tertiary education.

- *School learnings*

If the right to education should be right to the education "best suited to prepare the children of the world for the responsibilities of freedom", as reads the UNESCO's Constitution (Article I.2.b)[153], basic school education should provide learnings necessary for the development of all dimensions of the personality and to the quality of a *human* life. It should include, as priority matters, physical education, health education, including sexuality, appropriate education for parenthood[154], aesthetic education, education for human rights as Ethics of Humanity.

With regard to new learnings required by the evolving nature of the content of the object of the right to education, the most uncontroversial example, perhaps, is digital literacy, including to learn how to navigate the Internet's virtually infinite but dangerous ocean (see 2.3.8).

Furthermore, everything children and adolescents may want to know and ask in a classroom is part of the 'program', no matter how uncomfortable it may be for teachers when they are not educated and trained for the fullness of their mission. As wisely remarked the Colombian Constitutional Court (*T-337/95*)[155]: "Questions students ask in the classroom and teachers' answers belong to the education process".

- *Lifelong learning*

Lifelong education or learning is an ancient insight that has become a political principle. The Education 2030 Framework for Action states: "The right to education begins at birth and continues throughout life; therefore, the concept of *lifelong learning* guides SDG4-Education 2030." (para. 15)[156]

Nowadays, we know that human beings' educability changes, as they mature, but never ceases. The ability, need and desire to learn, have no age or satiety. It begins in the mother's womb and ends in the womb of the earth.

The normative integrity of the right to education is not, therefore, met by public school systems designed according to assumptions overtaken by the evolution of knowledge, technologies and societies.

- *Other remarks*

It should be noted that the right to education also entails the official recognition of the studies successfully accomplished, without which its *effet utile* (useful effect) would be impaired. A number of legal instruments have been adopted, at international level, on the recognition of studies, qualifications and diplomas.

Last but not least, when the human rights interdependence is lost from sight, the right to education may be a chimera...

2.3.6 Right to a rightful school

School is so relevant for the implementation of the right to education that it is frequently confused with right to school. It is eminently right to school, but not to whichever school.

School is an institution that has configured modern times but, while the world and most societies have changed profoundly, its 'soul' remained in the 19th century. The average school falls short, in general, of meeting the needs, possibilities and challenges of new times, having become, over the past few decades, a permanent refurbishment yard, a cemetery of innovations, an incinerator of pedagogical literature … This is why it is criticised so much, especially since the 1960s. The most disturbing criticism of school is that of its principal 'customers' – children and adolescents – reflecting their *malaise* (unease) and even revolt. They *feel* that they are entitled to a different school. And they are right.

When children go to school, for the first time, their eyes twinkle but, from year to year, the desire blanches … giving way to disliking school. School underperformance and indiscipline are chronic symptoms of rejection of the authoritarian, reductive and anachronistic logic of most schools we know. The 'school success' costs, to a large extent, the renouncement to the sense of learning, and may induce the habit of renouncing to sense in general, generating conformism and passiveness, so that its human costs are no less disturbing than the individual and social costs of 'school failure'.

Here is the 'mortal sin' of school: it tends to atrophy the desire and joy to learn, so betraying its *raison d'être* (reason to be). It is an illegitimate, irrational, pathological school:

- when it keeps working following assumptions invalidated by the progress of knowledge, underestimating the value of diversity, sensitivity and creativity in learning as an emotional, cultural, social, phenomenon;

- when it is captured by the 'needs of the economy' and the imperative of 'competitiveness', to the detriment of learnings fundamental to both the development of the personality and the vitality of democracies;

- when their pantagruelic programmes tend to schooling the life of children and adolescents, treating them as 'school animals', with the 'good pupil' being the obedient, decorative pet piece, and the 'bad pupil' the wild, disruptive, ugly piece;

- when it is content with fictions of learning that cost the renunciation of so much joy of living and other possibilities of being, and from so much school the feeling that lingers most is nostalgia for lost years of life;

- when it does not do everything it should do, and does badly much of what it does, because it is only 'worth' what counts for 'the grade' and anything goes to get the 'good grades' that count;

- when it assumes that the objectivity of learning assessment is guaranteed by tests quantified down to the most ridiculous tenths;

- when it is more *suffered* as obligation and necessary evil than *enjoyed* as a right and desired good;

- when it contributes to cultural anorexia, mental desertification, civic indifference, depersonalising mimicry, frivolity of existence;

- when it is a cause of frustration leading to indiscipline, rebellion, aggression, destruction, delinquency and even murder and suicide;

- when it is unable to compete with the media and other undesirable influences;

- when it shares so much responsibility for so many personal and social evils.

This criticism is not a manifestation of a gratuitous and sterile radicalism, it is laid down in documents approved by Ministers of Education, as well as in international and national reports published in recent decades.

Furthermore, most schools are available only for children and adolescents, closing after regular teaching hours. This is a waste of facilities and resources.

Such a school is not yet a rightful school.

Does the school institution have a future?

One hardly conceives of societies without an institution like school, which remains necessary to Civilisation. For having a future, however, it must undergo a transfiguration. A rightful school is a community, humanistic, desired school.

- *Rightful school* is an institution transfigured by the principle of lifelong education, where new generations meet to learn fundamental values and knowledge, but also where adult people may willingly go, outside their working hours, to learn whatever they need or desire, with available and able professionals. It should offer to parents, for example, the possibility to learn how to better love and educate their children.

  Such a school is a *community school,* inclusive in a broad sense, i.e. open to the diversity of ages, needs and interests of the plurality of the subjects of the right to education[157].

- *Rightful school* is a school passionate about the value of liberty, driven by the culture of the various dimensions of personality, where children, adolescents, young and adults can enjoy learning what matters for a life with dignity, amiability, creativity, in community, and not just what is needed to 'make a living'.

Such a school is a *humanistic school,* that is, not captured by interests that alienate it, but consistent with its moral mission and civilisational responsibility.

- *Rightful school* is a safe, healthy, comfortable, beautiful setting, concerned with what each child and adolescent is and can be, as well as with all factors and conditions of their ability and willingness to learn. A setting where those who get there like to be, because they feel respected and valued in their worth, dignity and uniqueness.

  Such a school is a welcoming, *desired school* – without failure, without indiscipline, without violence – a greenhouse of humanity and future.

Schools like this will be Palaces of the Right to Education.

2.3.7 Right to admirable education professionals

For children, mothers and fathers are persons unique in the world, but they may not be the best persons of the world ... They are not chosen but can learn to love and to educate. In any case, one can choose, educate and train education professionals who are mediators of the best a society and the humankind have to give to their children (see 3.10). However, education professions, teachers in particular, suffer from a chronic problem of identity. What professions should they be?

The identity of the professions with the greatest social relevance, responsibility and recognition has a specific density resulting from the composition of their triple identity content: knowledge to be applied, values to be respected, qualities to be cultivated. Determining the identity content of education professions must reflect their differences and requirements.

The very identity of the teaching profession, in particular, does not truly lie in the 'knowledge to be taught' or in 'knowing how to teach', that is, it does not consist only in "what teachers are expected to know and be able to do". Not only should they know *to do things right,* but also *to do the right things.* They should consider themselves and be considered as *professionals of the right to education and of the pedagogical communication,* the centre of gravity of their professionalism being their *personality.*

In other words: Being a teacher should be a *knowing-being-and-communicating-pedagogically,* that is, to know how to be the persons they should be and know how to communicate with the legitimacy and the quality of the right to education.

Given the present general degradation of its professional and social status, as well as the revolution of technologies of information and communication, there is reason for the question: Does the teaching profession have a future? If school has a future, the profession has a future as well, but what kind of education professions needs the future?

The answer may be inspired by the three famous interrogations of the Paul Gauguin painting, which teachers should also ask themselves, nowadays: *Where do we come from? What are we? Where are we going?*

The following responses are proposed:

- Teachers began to be *professionals of learning.*
- Now they are becoming rather *professionals of learning to learn.*
- In the future, they will be, above all, *professionals of learning to be.*

The educational relation – especially during childhood and the first years of schooling – is always intensely interpersonal. A teacher 'teaches' more the person he or she is than what s(he) knows, as one reads in pedagogical literature. This is his or her most unforgettable lesson.

Therefore, in education there is not professional quality without personal qualities: emotional, moral, intellectual qualities, of affectivity and amiability, of attention to the alterity and valuation of the diversity, of intelligence of the human historicity and perfectibility. They are qualities that arouse respect and admiration, exerting a profound and resonant influence. That is why an educator is not whoever, but who is it, who communicates and communicates himself or herself affectively, freely, serenely, luminously, admirably, unforgettably ...

As a consequence, here is a vision of the quintessence and future of the teaching profession: Teachers – and education professionals in general – will be *professionals of example.* Example stands for education professions as empathy for health professions, and the sentiment of justice for legal professions. In no other profession is it so central, essential and professional. A classical theme in the history of the pedagogic thought, example lies at the core of the professionalism in education. Educational exemplarity should be understood as an exceptional personification of a blend of qualities, values and knowledge. It begins with the way of being, speaking, treating, and has multiple resonances: moral, intellectual, civic, aesthetic, etc. This is the most profound and distinct professional identity, in education.

For the education professions – especially the teaching profession – to be what they should be, with a professional and social status commensurate with their exceptionality – two factors may be decisive: the cultivation of their ethical dimension and self-regulation statute.

- *Professional Ethics is the soul of professionalism.* It expresses the quintessence of a professional culture. A high ethical profile affirms the identity and cultivates the dignity, credibility and prestige of a profession. Is there a higher professional priority? And who better than teachers should know, and more interest should have, in taking care of the Value and the Values of their profession, which may be considered as the most ethical one?

- *Self-regulation is an insignia of professionality.* It can have decisive repercussions on the conception of the identity and attractiveness of the teaching profession; on the selection, education, training and evaluation of teachers; on their professional and social status, self-esteem and motivation; on the mission of school as an institution of humanisation; and on the quality of education. Professional self-regulation may be a bridge between the present and future of the teaching profession.

2.3.8 Right of access to Internet

Human right is an open concept, as above said. Right of access to Internet is an example of an emerging right.

The right of access to Internet can be derived from the right "to enjoy the benefits of scientific progress and its applications" (Article 15 of the International Covenant on Economic, Social and Cultural Rights), as well as from the right to "freedom to seek, receive and impart information and ideas of all kinds, regardless of frontiers", in any form (Article 19 of the International Covenant on Civil and Political Rights, replicated in Article 13 of the Convention on the Rights of the Child).

The Committee on the Rights of the Child adopted a General Comment 25 "on children's rights in relation to the digital environment" (CRC/C/GC/25, 2 March 2021)[158]. It recommends *inter alia*:

> 9. The right to non-discrimination requires that States Parties ensure that all children have equal and effective access to the digital environment in ways that are meaningful for them. States Parties should take all measures necessary to overcome digital exclusion. [...]
>
> ...
>
> 54. ... States Parties should not intentionally obstruct or enable other actors to obstruct the supply of electricity, cellular networks or Internet connectivity in any geographical area, whether in part or as a whole, which can have the effect of hindering a child's access to information and communication.
>
> ...
>
> 99. The digital environment can greatly enable and enhance children's access to high-quality inclusive education, including reliable resources for formal, non-formal, informal, peer-to-peer and self-directed learning. [...]
>
> ...

> 104. States Parties should ensure that digital literacy is taught in schools, as part of basic education curricula, from the preschool level and throughout all school years, and that such pedagogies are assessed on the basis of their results. [...]

The Human Rights Council has adopted, since 2012, several Resolutions on "The promotion, protection and enjoyment of human rights on the Internet".

The world pandemic has made clear how instrumental to the right to education the right to Internet is, which implies digital literacy. The European Parliament published, in 2021, a study on "Internet access as a fundamental right: Exploring aspects of connectivity"[159]. The European Commission (European Union) has adopted a "Digital Education Action Plan 2021-2027 – Resetting education and training for the digital age" (SWD(2020) 209 final)[160].

2.3.9 Right to an effective remedy

As above said, a general (customary) principle of justice is that the violation of a right must be remediable. The right of appeal is also a human right. As reads the Universal Declaration of Human Rights (Article 8)[161]: "Everyone has the right to an effective remedy by the competent national tribunals for acts violating the fundamental rights granted him by the constitution or by law."

Violations of the right to education – on grounds of discrimination, disciplinary sanctions, abusive indoctrination, omission or otherwise – should be liable to appeal to national courts and possibly to international bodies, such as the UN Committees and the European Court of Human Rights. There is a vast Case Law on the right to education at international and national levels.

Students' Ombudspersons have been established in many Universities. It would be highly desirable to have National Students' Ombudspersons with an extended mandate covering the whole school population.

In concluding

The implementation of the right to education requires a Right to Education Pedagogy and Policy, so understood:

- *Right to Education Pedagogy* is a theoretical-methodological conception of education illuminated by the Ethics of the Right to Education and grounded in the Sciences of Education.

- *Right to Education Policy* is a vision of the implementation of Educational Rights whose main vectors are family, school and education professions, taking into account two principles deriving from International Human Rights Law: interdependence of the human rights of the subject of the right to education and their correlation with the rights of educators.

It should be added that, if 'sciences of education' are all knowledge disciplines which can contribute to the comprehension of the educational phenomenon and the improvement of education, they should notably include the following ones: International Education Law, Neuroscience of Education, Semiotics of Education, Aesthetics of Education. They are needed to examine the fundamental questions that the educational phenomenon raises and to identify Principles of General Methodology, i.e. valid for all kinds of education. They are also necessary to understand why the principle of all methods will always be the personality of educators.

In the history of the pedagogic thought, the new-born was sometimes compared to a soil to be cultivated or a clay to be shaped or a blackboard or a clean slate or blank canvas where education writes the *text* of much of his or her destiny. Education should be thought of and practiced as *Ars Magna* (Great Art) of dreaming and loving, reading and writing the 'human text'. *Divine art of invisibly sculpting the humanity of children.*

Chapter 3
Answering some questions

Readers of this book may be interested in answers – in light of the right to education – to some questions more familiar to public opinion and others, such as:

1. Is there acceptable corporal punishment in education?
2. Does homeschooling satisfy the right to education?
3. There is "compulsory" schooling, but may a right become obligation?
4. What should be covered by the gratuity of public school?
5. Are parents entitled to prevent children from attending a school subject matter?
6. May school regulations include rules on students' clothing and appearance?
7. Is school homework legitimate and beneficial?
8. What may be the place of religion in public schools?
9. Is privatisation of education compatible with International Education Law?

The following are more or less brief answers to these questions.

3.1 Is there acceptable corporal punishment in education?

Corporal punishment has been the traditional 'method' of education, passed down from generation to generation through well-known proverbs, with biblical 'authority' (*Proverbs*, 13:24: "He who spares his rod hates his son, but he who loves him takes care to chastise him")[162]. It is a long chapter in the history of education and of the violence between human beings. Its necessity remains ingrained in mentalities.

The incompatibility of corporal punishment with respect for the dignity and physical, moral and psychological integrity of children is already largely incorporated into the juridical and pedagogical conscience. The worst forms of violence towards children are virtually forbidden around the world. However, corporal punishment, in education, continues to be culturally and socially tolerated across geographical and cultural boundaries, in particular at home. Tribunals and Courts themselves still often invoke the Anglo-Saxon "reasonable chastisement" doctrine in support of a "right of correction", especially in the family.

Family should not continue to be the only social place where violence is not illegal. There are no lawful moderate acts of violence upon human beings, much less children. When parents hit their children *for love*, they grow learning that aggression or even killing may be a form of love.

Corporal punishment violates the Convention on the Rights of the Child and has been condemned by UN Committees and international and national Courts[163]. For example, it has been condemned by the European Court of Human Rights in the following classical Cases: *Tyrer v. the United Kingdom* (1978), *Campbell and Cosans v. the United Kingdom* (1982), *A. v. the United Kingdom* (1998) – after which the United Kingdom successively banned corporal punishment in public and private schools, as well as in family.

However, it is important not to understand "corporal punishment" in a fundamentalist way. A seemingly less affectionate physical contact between a mother or father and a little child, occasional and in a context of some tension and turbulence, should not be qualified as bodily harm or assault.

The relation of corporal punishment with emotional disturbances, malformation of moral conscience, decreased self-esteem, school failure, anti-social behaviour, etc. is well established. It is not only a problem of education but also a matter of public health and security, given its resonances in the entire society[164].

In any case, breaking the vicious circle of violence against children is not simply a legal issue nor just a pedagogical one. It involves all factors – cultural, social, economic, psychological, etc. – of the reproduction of violence between human beings.

A sanction is educational only if it does not physically assault or psychologically injure the sentiment of personal value and dignity and carries a sense of reparation and *self-revaluation.*

3.2 Does homeschooling satisfy the right to education?

It is generally understood that compulsory schooling means compulsory attendance at school. States Parties in the Convention on the Rights of the Child[165] undertake to: "Take measures to encourage regular attendance at schools and the reduction of drop-out rates." (Article 28.1.e) Nevertheless, International Education Law does not formally exclude the possibility of basic school education to be accomplished at home. In the US, for example, homeschooling is legal in all federal States. In Europe, it is legal in some countries. The European Court of Human Rights recognises States' margin of appreciation in this matter. The justifications invoked by parents may be gifted children, best quality of instruction at home, school insecurity. The most frequent, however, are convictions, religious or others.

Homeschooling is obviously justified for children who, for health reasons, cannot attend school, or for children of nomadic families or which, for professional reasons, are frequently moving, but does not satisfy the normative comprehensiveness of the object of the right to education.

Even though instruction of children may be well or even better achieved at home, the human right to education is not only right to instruction (or to whatever education), nor just an individual good, as noted the European Court. School is an institution where the new generations meet to learn common values, fundamental and other knowledge, as well as for experiencing and learning the coexistence of the cultural, social, individual diversity.

States have an obligation to protect the right to education of children against its 'expropriation' by families, if needed, and also have a legitimate interest in their education, as organs of the Common Good.

3.3 There is "compulsory" schooling, but may a right become an obligation?

Elementary/primary or basic education/school is "compulsory". This term raised a controversy in the Commission on Human Rights, during the drafting of the Universal Declaration but, as the Committee on Economic, Social and Cultural Rights recalled in its General Comment 11 (E/C.12/1999/4)[166]: "The element of compulsion serves to highlight the fact that neither parents, nor guardians, nor the State are entitled to treat as optional the decision as to whether the child should have access to primary education." (para. 6)

A human right is not necessarily jeopardised if an element of the content of its object is made compulsory, if this is a legitimate public interest not incompatible with respect for the substance of that right. Other examples of elements of human rights that sometimes are made compulsory are vaccination and voting[167]. Nevertheless, the principle of compulsory education still is sometimes questioned, in particular with regard to its duration.

In this respect, the Committee on Economic, Social and Cultural Rights has wisely observed in the abovementioned General Comment 11: "It should be emphasized, however, that the education offered must be adequate in quality, relevant to the child and must promote the realization of the child's other rights." (para. 6)

Indeed, what is at stake is less the obligation than the quality of education.

3.4 What should be covered by the gratuity of public school?

The right to education is the only human right with a formally free element: compulsory primary/basic education. The scope of the gratuity is undefined, however. And may be nullified by lateral means.

Gratuity of schooling may be limited to the direct costs of attending (enrolment and other payments) or include more costs. It is increasingly considered that it should tend to cover all its costs and conditions[168]. The "Principles and Guidelines on the Implementation of Economic, Social and Cultural Rights in the African Charter on Human and Peoples' Rights", adopted by the African Commission on Human and Peoples' Rights, include as "minimum Core Obligations" (71.b)[169]:

> To implement policies to eliminate or reduce the costs of attending primary school which include the provision of stipends, providing free or subsidised uniforms (or lifting of uniform requirements), provision of free textbooks, provision of free or subsidised transportation or free school meals to encourage the attendance of poor children at school.

There is international and national Case Law converging in the same sense.

As regards higher levels of the school system, attendance should be facilitated by all means as long as it is not free too.

In fact, one measure to promote school attendance and prevent drop-out is – along with policies against poverty, relevant school programmes, a respectful and welcoming school environment, a valued and socially esteemed teaching profession – to make compulsory schooling truly free, including free transport, free textbooks and other learning materials, as well as free food, free health care and other supporting measures.

3.5 Are parents entitled to prevent children from attending a school subject matter?

Some school programs raise sometimes objections from parents, alleging their convictions. It is claimed that children's education is their "fundamental right", often invoking the Universal Declaration of Human Rights (Article 26.3).

A legal instrument is a *living* document, as the European Court of Human Rights, for example, sometimes observes[170]. It should be interpreted and applied taking into account its *travaux préparatoires,* the context and evolution of Law (systematic principle), as well as the teleological principle, i.e. the "object and purpose" of the agreed normativity, as reads Article 31.1 of the Vienna Convention on the Law of Treaties (1969)[171].

There is much international and national jurisprudence converging on this conclusion: There is no valid "conscientious objection" against the right of children to the normative integrity of their right to education, internationally recognised and protected. The Committee on the Rights of Persons with Disabilities observed in its General Comment 4 "on the right to inclusive education" (CRPD/C/GC/4, 25 November 2016)[172] that "education is the right of the individual learner and not, in the case of children, the right of a parent or caregiver. Parental responsibilities in this regard are subordinate to the rights of the child" (Article 10.a). A "fundamental right" of parents concerning the education of children would not be compatible with *their* human right to education[173]. As the Parliamentary Assembly of the Council of Europe has stated in its Resolution 2253 (2019) on "Sharia, the Cairo Declaration and the European Convention on Human Rights"[174], "where human rights are concerned, there is no room for religious or cultural exceptions" (para. 9).

Therefore, if conflicts arise between Family and State, regarding children's education, what is really at stake is neither a Family's right nor a State's right; but the right of the child to education. It must be protected both against State, in case of attempted totalitarian appropriation of children, or against Family, if the physical, moral and psychological integrity or the development of children are at risk. And not by replacing one totalitarianism with another.

Children need the protection and guidance of adults, of course, first and foremost of their parents, for growing and learning to enjoy their rights. By guiding them, they do it naturally in accordance with their values and convictions, but they have not the right to impose them, disregarding the rights of the child. They only have the grave responsibility to be humanely exemplary. This is the most legitimate and profound influence adults can exert over children.

3.6 May school regulations include rules on student clothing and appearance?

School communities need regulations defining the rights and duties of their members. As far as students are concerned, they sometimes include rules about their clothing and appearance. In private schools, such rules may not be challenged, as attendance is a choice, but in public schools they are controversial.

Regarding school uniforms, there are arguments for and against. They are frequent in private institutions but have almost disappeared from public schools. Controversial are rules interfering with individual freedom, such as: clothing, use of fashion accessories, hairstyle, expression of opinions, sexuality, private life.

Rights of students (and also of teachers) may be subject to legitimate restrictions, compatible with respect for their human rights whose exercise is not incompatible with respect for the rights of others, the safety of the school environment, the fulfilment of the school's mission and the values of Public Order. This is not the case of regulatory norms conditioning the legitimate expression of personality, much less interfering in private life, as if educational institutions were places of exception to respect for constitutional values and rights.

There is a varied and rich jurisprudence on these matters pronounced by the Constitutional Court of Colombia and several US High Courts, for example, according to which the general principle concerning these matters should be the freedom of expression of personality and the rights it entails.

3.7 Is school homework legitimate and beneficial?

School homework is still a vigorous tradition, and the idea of its abolition is not popular. However, in light of the Convention on the Rights of the Child, it is not legitimate, for the following main reasons:

- it encroaches on other rights, such as the rights to private and familial life, to rest, to leisure, to play, to cultural life, not to mention the case of children who have to work to help family;

- it may be discriminatory insofar as not every child has 'school at home', i.e. favourable spaces, needed resources, as well as parents able and available to help do it;

- it harms on the harmonious development of children and adolescents and may become disruptive of the familial peace, when it arouses resistance and motivates punishment, thus aggravating school disgust.

In addition, school homework does not have proven indisputable usefulness. On the contrary, it is a factor, for example, of obesity, increasing of diabetes associated with a sedentary lifestyle, and myopia.

In short: The right to education does not legitimise schooling the life that children and adolescents should be free to live outside of it. School has the obligation to do everything incumbent on it during the long schooling days and years. This does not prevent, however, a teacher from suggesting activities at home that children or adolescents may be willing to do.

3.8 What may be the place of religion in public schools?

The separation between State and religion is an aspect of the modernisation of societies, when the principle of State secularity emerged, which means non-confessionalism or religious neutrality. It is a typically French principle, instituted by the Law of Separation of Church and State, on 9 December 1905, commemorated (in France) as the Day of Secularism since 2015[175].

International Human Rights Law does not exclude a special relationship of the State with a traditional religion having deeper cultural roots in a country. It even yet admits the existence of a State Religion. In any case, indoctrination – religious or anti-religious – is excluded.

The principle of non-indoctrination – that is also an imperative of compulsory education – applies not only to religious education but to the entire public school learning. As representatives of State's authority, teachers are subject to a duty of reserve which may entail legitimate restrictions on their freedom of expression. The principle of non-indoctrination is the most widely respectful of the interests at stake in public school, namely:

- the convictions of all parents;
- the right to education of every student;
- the diversity and pluralism in democracy.

Non-confessionalism of public school does not exclude the possibility of religious education, under certain conditions, particularly the following:

- it should be taken in charge by the religions concerned, as teachers should never be obliged to provide it;

- it should never be compulsory, and the exemption may be requested by parents or legal guardians, or by students themselves, from a determined age, variable.

It should be noted, however, that the possibility of exemption from attending religious education classes, in public school, is not free from unwanted or even unacceptable effects of discrimination, stigmatisation and violation of privacy.

Compulsory instruction about religion as a cultural phenomenon is not incompatible with the principle of non-confessionalism. In effect, religion is one of the most influential vectors of Civilisation – sometimes negative, sometimes positive – and the history and culture of every country has a religious imprint. Moreover, knowledge of the religious phenomenon and of the plurality of its expressions may contribute to the cultivation of the freedom of thought, conscience and religion, as well as to a culture of tolerance. Anything that can contribute to making human beings better is welcome.

The principle of non-confessionalism covers other aspects of public school life, about which there is a significant national and international Case Law. Although with some variations, its general sense is that are not compatible with the principles of non-confessionalism and non-indoctrination in public schools:

- mandatory acts or events with religious content, such as prayers and religious ceremonies;

- presence of religious symbols at school, although admitting that State might have a margin of appreciation;

- use of clothing or symbols with strong religious or ideological connotations, even though teachers' and students' positions are not similar, and a general ban may not be advisable or even acceptable.

The use of school facilities for activities of a religious nature, outside of their regular operation, is not, in principle, incompatible with the principle of State's non-confessionalism.

Non-confessionalism does not mean an impossible moral neutrality of education, of course. The Rule of Law is, nowadays, driven by constitutional values that schools – public and private – must respect and promote. They are, above all, the values of the Ethics of Human Rights as Ethics of Humanity. States Parties to International Education Law are committed to education for human rights – the sole legitimate indoctrination in public schools.

3.9 Is privatisation of education compatible with International Education Law?

Since the 19th century, education in the Western world has been a typical function of State, almost a monopoly, through a public school system to fulfil the constitutional and legal imperative of compulsory schooling. Freedom of education/instruction was first recognised in Constitutions as an element of the freedom of expression proclaimed by the French Declaration of 1789 (Article 11).

With the advent of International Human Rights Law, the relationship between the right to education and the liberties of education included in its international provisions has been discussed. The possibility of conflict has increased since the late 1980s, with the wave of expansion of private education – and privatisation of parts of public education systems – that has risen on all continents.

In knowledge-based societies and a technology-driven world, the education demand has extraordinarily increased, but the expansion of digital technologies as tools for learning has been predominantly explored by neoliberalism that has ridden Globalisation.

For the sake of clarification, liberty of education, liberalisation of education and privatisation of education should be distinguished. The following distinction is proposed:

- *Liberty of education* is the traditional liberty of parents relating to the education of children, as well as the liberty of private education as a dimension of freedom of thought, conscience, religion, as well as of freedom of economic initiative.

- *Liberalisation of education* is a policy of opening up the provision of education services to the private sector, including possible incentives for investment such as land transfers, tax benefits or even funding.

- *Privatisation of education* occurs when public education facilities and services are transferred to the private sector, with possible effects of commercialisation of the right to education.

States may contract to private sector ancillary services for public institutions, or finance private entities for the supplementary provision of essential services. This is the case of Public-Private Partnerships (PPPs), sometimes regarded as a kind of 'Columbus egg' combining the best of two worlds: the public and the private.

Two typical modalities of public-private relationship, in the education field, are Charter Schools (schools under contract) and Vouchers (education checks), originating in the US and reproduced in other countries. Vouchers are particularly controversial.

Education/School Voucher is a payment title for attendance of a chosen school, delivered to families or directly to schools on their behalf by public authorities (or even by private entities). Voucher programs may be focused or universal, that is, intended only for a few categories of students or for everyone, and be used in a public or private school.

Vouchers' advocates argue that they provide disadvantaged families, in more degraded city areas or rural areas, with the freedom to choose for their children a private school better than a public school; and that, by stimulating competitiveness between schools (not only between private and public schools, but also between public schools themselves), they also promote the quality of education in general. It is assumed that the better a school, the more students it attracts and more funding it gets (in US).

The main argument of opponents is that Vouchers' policies amount to a form of diversion of public resources into the private sector, to the detriment of improving the quality of public school. Another argument against the Vouchers policy in the US is that it violates the principle of separation between State and religion (First Amendment of the Constitution), as they are often used to attend religious schools, including those teaching Creationism, which rejects the theory of evolution. Some US Courts have ruled that Voucher programs are unconstitutional. The Supreme Court has admitted its constitutionality under certain conditions.

The private initiative can have a positive impact on the implementation of the right to education: increasing the availability of educational institutions, especially when the public offer is insufficient, is beneficial, in principle; the presence of credible foreign education institutions is positive; diversification of education on offer may help to raise its quality.

However, the private provision of essential education services may also have considerable negative effects, if it is not properly regulated and supervised. In addition to possible effects of commercialisation of the right to education – causing discrimination and impoverishment of its integrity and of the heritage of diversity – it may contribute to the creation of a two-track school system: one for the rich (private schools) and another for the poor (public schools), becoming a factor of segregation and stratification.

In 2019, the *Abidjan Principles on the human rights obligations of States to provide public education and to regulate private involvement in education*[176] were adopted, after having been drafted by international experts during approximately three-years, in a process of broad global consultation, with the support of several NGOs. They are 10 "Overarching Principles", more 97 "Guiding Principles", approved by a final Conference in Abidjan (Ivory Coast), on 13 February[177].

According to International Education Law and much of its jurisprudential and doctrinal interpretation:

- International Education Law excludes both the complete privatisation of education and a public monopoly, but States have an obligation to establish and to develop a public school system with a free compulsory component.

- States should give priority to the funding of public education, both at the national level and in their co-operation with other States, as well as in development aid programmes of international organisations of which they are members.

- International Education Law does not prescribe or prohibit public funding of private education institutions but, if there is funding, it must be done without discrimination.

- The contractualisation of the provision of essential education services by private actors should be temporary and never contribute to sustaining for-profit institutions.

- As education is a human right and a public good, States are entitled to impose to private actors public service obligations, in particular with regard to affordability, quality, equity, neutrality, continuity.

- States should adopt and supervise compliance with regulations ensuring that private provision of essential education services meets international and national standards on the right to education.

Whereas the private provision of public services required by human rights is not incompatible with International Human Rights Law, States are always responsible, legally and politically, individually and collectively, for guaranteeing their provision. States' functions may change, but their responsibility should be never privatised.

The right to education must be protected against the liberties of education treating children and adolescents, in particular, as 'property', 'objects', 'recipients', 'consumers', that is, against its expropriation both by a liberty of education exercised as a refuge of the traditional "right of education" – amounting to a kind of moral (re)privatisation of human beings – or used as a 'Trojan Horse' for the commercialisation of the right to education.

Summing up:

The traditional doctrine of the liberty of education is more concerned with the authority of adults than with the liberty of children. It cares more about the liberty of indoctrination than about the liberty of thinking.

There should be no liberty of education against the right to education. The liberty that is truly at stake in education, both at home and in school, public or private, is the liberty of the subject of the right to education, especially of children, adolescents and young, to learn and to learn liberty with liberty.

In the Biblical Gospels, there is a scene where Jesus Christ chases sellers of oxen, sheep, pigeons and money changers from the temple of Jerusalem, telling them: "Don't make my Father's house a business house" (John, 2.14). In education too, there is the sacred and the market. There is the *temple* of the human right to education, the *sanctum sanctorum* (holiest place) of which is a normative core consubstantial to human dignity that must be safeguarded against any transaction. Around, chapels exist that may be approached by diverse services providers, duly accredited and supervised. Outside the temple, a variety of knowledge may be freely sold and bought.

In concluding

The Uruguayan poet Mario Benedetti wrote: "When we thought we had all the answers, suddenly all the questions changed."[178]

The questions above formulated are not all new, but they have been answered in the light of the answer to a radically new one, posed in the Introduction: *By what right to educate*?

The human right to education is a new theoretical-normative framework for thinking and acting. By freeing education from its traditional naturalistic and sociological postulates, it dissolves chronic problems, such as school failure and indiscipline, creating the conditions for eliminating their causes; it indicates principles for solving others, such as the love of children, the exercise of authority and the quality of education; it raises new questions, notably the meta-question of the legitimacy of education.

The right to education has then a revolutionary significance.

Conclusion
Revolution of the Right to Education

The human species has of itself a positively or negatively exaggerated image...

Man is an animal whose distinctiveness has been described manyfold. In light of the above proposed conception of human dignity, the human animal may be qualified as *historical* (in becoming, perfectible), *semiotic* (producer and consumer of symbols/signs), *rational* (capable of thinking, imagining, creating), *moral* (needing values to live, to suffer, to die), *pedagogical* (because of having to learn the *humaneness*).

Man is a *pedagogical animal* because he is born as a *de-natured animal* that, without education, becomes a *dis-figured human being,* as illustrated by cases of so-called 'wild children' or 'wolf children'. Education is a phenomenon of *human (con)figuration* that amounts to a *second birth* for a *second nature.* It is because they are so radically educable that human beings are able both to ascend to the heights of the sublimity of moral, intellectual, artistic, genius, or to descend to the depths and darkness of a cruelty of which no other animal species is capable.[179]

Each human being is, therefore, born without a *raison d'être* (reason for being) but has many reasons to be as (s)he is. Of how many needs and influences, sentiments and ideas, distresses and revolts, desires and dreams, a human being is made up ... This is one reason why life imprisonment and death penalty are unjust, inhumane, primitive punishments.

With the neuroscientific revolution of recent decades, we are beginning to understand how education has the repercussions it has, visible and invisible, on individual and collective life. The species' children become *truly human* insofar as their basic bio-emotional needs are satisfied and their interiority is cultivated by the purest seeds of truth, goodness, beauty ...

Here's why the human species is not the worst animal species: it can learn to be infinitely better. Education is its *Philosopher's Stone.*

Globally regarded, however, the world of education still looks like the Ptolemaic astronomical system in the late Middle Ages: In the galaxy of education, the sun keeps moving around the earth ... Saturated with reforms, the paradigm of the traditional right of education is exhausted. That is why a revolution in education has often been called for since the end of the 19th century, at least.

What educational revolution is needed?

A truly educational revolution is not merely an instrumental, scientific-technological one, *PowerPoint revolution...* It must be, first and foremostly, a normative revolution, that is, consistent with the values and principles that should really inspire and guide education, both in families and in schools, public and private.

There is no timeless ideal education, but there is an ideal of education in every epoch, open to the lights of the deepening of science and conscience, for the historical perfecting of the humankind, through its children. The New Education Movement bequeathed to us a heritage of values and principles with revolutionary potential, to which the normative content of the human right to education gave legal form and strength.

What is the revolutionary significance of the right to education?

Revolution is a term frequently used to qualify the advent of human rights, as we saw. We know why human rights and the rights of the child are revolutionary advancements: The human person has been consecrated as the ethical-juridical supreme value – with dignity and rights recognised and protected by International Human Rights Law and in the legal orders of most States – and the child has been fully recognised as a person, equal to adults by dignity and rights.

Revolution of the Right to Education is not a voluntarist, rhetorical proclamation. The Report of UNICEF (United Nations International Children's Emergency Fund) on *The State of the World's Children 1999*[180] included a section on "The education revolution". It affirmed:

> If access to quality learning is one guiding light of this revolution, the other is child rights. In Article 28, the Convention on the Rights of the Child established the right of all children, without discrimination, to education. The Convention also provides a framework by which the quality of that education must be assessed. [...]
> The education revolution is reshaping the edifice of education. Under its aegis, schools must become zones of creativity, safety and stimulation for children, with safe water and decent sanitation, with motivated teachers and relevant curricula, where children are respected and learn to respect others. (p. 21-22)

The right to education is the 'telescope' of a Copernican revolution that is simply the corollary of its normative content, amounting to a paradigm shift: The *Paradigm of the Right to Education* means a movement from the *Paradigm of the Right of Education* to the *Paradigm of Rightful Education*.

Consequently, the necessary educational revolution does not consist just of making school education available and accessible all over the world, so that all children can become literate and have some preparation to 'earn a living'. This must remain a priority, of course, because it is still a distant goal, especially for girls and millions of girls and boys who are struggling to survive on every continent. However, a real revolution is not merely quantitative. The Revolution of the Right to Education – as a new right to a new education – is a qualitative breakthrough, the nature of which has been identified and characterized above.

The Revolution of the Right to Education means, after all, the rupture already envisaged by the two most influential UNESCO's Reports, so far, prepared by International Commissions: *Learning to Be: The world of education today and tomorrow* (Faure Report, 1972) and *Learning: The treasure within* (Delors Report, 1996). The Faure Report strived to rescue the profound humanist sense of education from its economist instrumentalisation. The Delors Report shared the main concerns of the Faure Report, mostly the trend to marketisation of education, and reaffirmed its principal ideas, in particular the paramountcy of education as an end in itself, encapsulated in its most known sentence: "Education throughout life is based on four pillars: learning to know, learning to do, learning to live together and learning to be." The title of Jacques Delors presentation of the Report is telling: "Education: the necessary Utopia". According to the Report, it is about an "ethical imperative", namely: "the ultimate societal aims of education should never obscure the primacy of the human individual and the ideals proclaimed by the international community when the United Nations was founded"[181].

Put in a nutshell: The Revolution of the Right to Education – like every true revolution in the world of human and social relations – is about children' and adolescents' *seizing power* and *empowerment.*

- *Seizing the power* of their right to education as right to free, full and harmonious development of their personality. It means *liberation* from the *right of education.*

- *Empowerment* through the culture of the most human aptitudes and humanistic values. It means right to a *Rightful Education.*

This is the *normative radicalism* of the human right to education. A still much distant ideal, but the only hope for the humankind.

The revolutionary significance of the right to education may not seem evident, especially for people living in societies where one apparently *breathes* human rights, but if we take a look at the realities and some perversities of family and school education around us and all over the world ... at education amounting to sequestration of the *soul* of children and peoples ... at the indecent leaders 'democratically' elected ... at the atrocities committed in the name of deities and their 'prophets'... at everything humans beings continue to do to each other...

The human species still lives in the age of caves, now digital caves... How long can it survive the wastage of *possibles* for its perfectibility?

Human rights institute limits that need to be learnt and they open possibles to the liberty to be. The right to education is right to learn both the *limits* of the finitude of the species, which inscribe in its children their ethical identity, and the *possibles* of the infinitude of the essential human perfectibility.

Possible is a philosophical multifaceted category. There are genetic, political, ethical, aesthetic, pedagogical *possibles*. The *Pedagogical Possible* is rooted in the Genetic Possible, calls for the Political Possible, believes in the Ethical Possible and dreams of the Aesthetic Possible. It is the inexhaustible harvest of the human species' perfectibility and uniqueness of its members.

Right to education is *Right to the Possible* – that does not become reality without struggle. The struggle for the right to education will be a long-lasting struggle, because:

- Basic human rights are still lacking for the great majority of human beings, especially children.
- Schools are lacking and tens of millions of children are lacking in schools because they must work or are forced to be involved in the wars of adults, or because of other disgraceful causes.
- The right to education is lacking at home and in schools, because loving children is necessary, but not any love is pedagogical; education is necessary, but not any education is legitimate; school is necessary, but it is not yet, in general, rightful school.

The world will not be an empire of human rights while States are not realms of human rights, but States will not be realms of human rights while families and schools are not homelands of children's rights.

One says that the wealth of nations are their peoples. The treasure of peoples lies in their children. It is in the bodies, hearts and minds of children that parents and peoples should sow the joys of their future. Children are the Utopia of Humankind. The map and the compass of this Utopia is the right to education as right to learn, to learn to learn, to learn to be human – equal, free, different, better.

The Revolution of the Right to Education could be poetised in an astronomic metaphor: Education should not be centred either in the *earth of the adults* or in the *sun of the childhood,* but rather visioned in the *universe of the human rights* where there are not majors and minors, parents and children, teachers and pupils, but *persons* equal by dignity and rights. As a consequence, the *pedagogical reason* is no longer the *biological reason* of the Family nor the *political reason* of the State, but the *Ethical Reason of the Subject* – open to the sublime utopias of the Possible…

The Revolution of the Right to Education – in resonance with the Revolution of Human Rights and the Revolution of the Rights of the Child – will mean the political-pedagogical breaking of the vicious circle of the historical and psychological *cloning* of the coming generations by the older ones, driven by the human compulsion and 'divine' temptation of parents to 'create' children "in their image and likeness". This revolutionary significance is deeply and beautifully intuited in the well-known and luminous verses of Khalil Gibran, a Lebanese American philosopher, writer and artist (*The Prophet,* 1923)[182]:

> And a woman who held a babe against her bosom said,
> "Speak to us of Children".
> And he said:
> Your children are not your children,
> they are the sons and daughters of Life's longing for itself.
> They come through you but not from you,

> and though they are with you, yet they belong not to you.
> You may give them your love but not your thoughts,
> for they have their own thoughts.
> You may house their bodies but not their souls,
> for their souls dwell in the house of tomorrow,
> which you cannot visit, not even in your dreams.
> You may strive to be like them but seek not to make them like you,
> for life goes not backward nor tarries with yesterday.

The world is made by human beings and human beings are their names, their faces, their bodies, and everything their lives and education generate inside themselves. We are not born human, we have to learn to be so. Education is the greatest human power and responsibility. It is not a magical power, but the human species has no greater power to take care of itself – of its emotions, sentiments, ideas, ideals, destiny…

To be or not to be a human right – here is the question regarding the future of education and of our Humanity.

Appendix 1
Main universal normative framework of the right to education

A1.1

Universal Declaration of Human Rights

United Nations, 1948

Article 26

1. Everyone has the right to education. Education shall be free, at least in the elementary and fundamental stages. Elementary education shall be compulsory. Technical and professional education shall be made generally available and higher education shall be equally accessible to all on the basis of merit.

2. Education shall be directed to the full development of the human personality and to the strengthening of respect for human rights and fundamental freedoms. It shall promote understanding, tolerance and friendship among all nations, racial or religious groups, and shall further the activities of the United Nations for the maintenance of peace.

3. Parents have a prior right to choose the kind of education that shall be given to their children.

A1.2

International Covenant on Economic, Social and Cultural Rights

United Nations, 1966

Article 13

1. The States Parties to the present Covenant recognize the right of everyone to education. They agree that education shall be directed to the full development of the

human personality and the sense of its dignity, and shall strengthen the respect for human rights and fundamental freedoms. They further agree that education shall enable all persons to participate effectively in a free society, promote understanding, tolerance and friendship among all nations and all racial, ethnic or religious groups, and further the activities of the United Nations for the maintenance of peace.

2. The States Parties to the present Covenant recognize that, with a view to achieving the full realization of this right:

a. Primary education shall be compulsory and available free to all;

b. Secondary education in its different forms, including technical and vocational secondary education, shall be made generally available and accessible to all by every appropriate means, and in particular by the progressive introduction of free education;

c. Higher education shall be made equally accessible to all, on the basis of capacity, by every appropriate means, and in particular by the progressive introduction of free education;

d. Fundamental education shall be encouraged or intensified as far as possible for those persons who have not received or completed the whole period of their primary education;

e. The development of a system of schools at all levels shall be actively pursued, an adequate fellowship system shall be established, and the material conditions of teaching staff shall be continuously improved.

3. The States Parties to the present Covenant undertake to have respect for the liberty of parents and, when applicable, legal guardians to choose for their children schools, other than those established by the public authorities, which conform to such minimum educational standards as may be laid down or approved by the State and to ensure the religious and moral education of their children in conformity with their own convictions.

4. No part of this article shall be construed so as to interfere with the liberty of individuals and bodies to establish and direct educational institutions, subject always to the observance of the principles set forth in paragraph I of this article and to the requirement that the education given in such institutions shall conform to such minimum standards as may be laid down by the State.

Article 14

Each State Party to the present Covenant which, at the time of becoming a Party, has not been able to secure in its metropolitan territory or other territories under its jurisdiction compulsory primary education, free of charge, undertakes, within two years, to work out and adopt a detailed plan of action for the progressive implementation, within a reasonable number of years, to be fixed in the plan, of the principle of compulsory education free of charge for all.

A1.3

Convention on the Rights of the Child

United Nations, 1989

Article 28

1. States Parties recognize the right of the child to education, and with a view to achieving this right progressively and on the basis of equal opportunity, they shall, in particular:

a. Make primary education compulsory and available free to all;

b. Encourage the development of different forms of secondary education, including general and vocational education, make them available and accessible to every child, and take appropriate measures such as the introduction of free education and offering financial assistance in case of need;

c. Make higher education accessible to all on the basis of capacity by every appropriate means;

d. Make educational and vocational information and guidance available and accessible to all children;

e. Take measures to encourage regular attendance at schools and the reduction of drop-out rates.

2. States Parties shall take all appropriate measures to ensure that school discipline is administered in a manner consistent with the child's human dignity and in conformity with the present Convention.

3. States Parties shall promote and encourage international cooperation in matters relating to education, in particular with a view to contributing to the elimination of ignorance and illiteracy throughout the world and facilitating access to scientific and technical knowledge and modern teaching methods. In this regard, particular account shall be taken of the needs of developing countries.

Article 29

1. States Parties agree that the education of the child shall be directed to:

a. The development of the child's personality, talents and mental and physical abilities to their fullest potential;

b. The development of respect for human rights and fundamental freedoms, and for the principles enshrined in the Charter of the United Nations;

c. The development of respect for the child's parents, his or her own cultural identity, language and values, for the national values of the country in which the child is living, the country from which he or she may originate, and for civilizations different from his or her own;

d. The preparation of the child for responsible life in a free society, in the spirit of understanding, peace, tolerance, equality of sexes, and friendship among all peoples, ethnic, national and religious groups and persons of indigenous origin;

e. The development of respect for the natural environment.

2. No part of the present Article or Article 28 shall be construed so as to interfere with the liberty of individuals and bodies to establish and direct educational institutions, subject always to the observance of the principle set forth in paragraph 1 of the present article and to the requirements that the education given in such institutions shall conform to such minimum standards as may be laid down by the State.

A1.4

Convention against Discrimination in Education

UNESCO, 1960

The General Conference of the United Nations Educational, Scientific and Cultural Organization, meeting in Paris from 14 November to 15 December 1960, at its eleventh session,

Recalling that the Universal Declaration of Human Rights asserts the principle of non-discrimination and proclaims that every person has the right to education,

Considering that discrimination in education is a violation of rights enunciated in that Declaration,

Considering that, under the terms of its Constitution, the United Nations Educational, Scientific and Cultural Organization has the purpose of instituting collaboration among the nations with a view to furthering for all universal respect for human rights and equality of educational opportunity,

Recognizing that, consequently, the United Nations Educational, Scientific and Cultural Organization, while respecting the diversity of national educational systems, has the duty not only to proscribe any form of discrimination in education but also to promote equality of opportunity and treatment for all in education,

Having before it proposals concerning the different aspects of discrimination in education, constituting item 17.1.4 of the agenda of the session,

Having decided at its tenth session that this question should be made the subject of an international convention as well as of recommendations to Member States,

Adopts this Convention on the fourteenth day of December 1960.

Article 1

1. For the purpose of this Convention, the term "discrimination" includes any distinction, exclusion, limitation or preference which, being based on race, colour, sex, language, religion, political or other opinion, national or social origin, economic condition or birth, has the purpose or effect of nullifying or impairing equality of treatment in education and in particular:

a. Of depriving any person or group of persons of access to education of any type or at any level;

b. Of limiting any person or group of persons to education of an inferior standard;

c. Subject to the provisions of article 2 of this Convention, of establishing or maintaining separate educational systems or institutions for persons or groups of persons; or

d. Of inflicting on any person or group of persons conditions which are incompatible with the dignity of man.

2. For the purposes of this Convention, the term "education" refers to all types and levels of education, and includes access to education, the standard and quality of education, and the conditions under which it is given.

Article 2

When permitted in a State, the following situations shall not be deemed to constitute discrimination, within the meaning of article 1 of this Convention:

a. The establishment or maintenance of separate educational systems or institutions for pupils of the two sexes, if these systems or institutions offer equivalent access to education, provide a teaching staff with qualifications of the same standard as well as school premises and equipment of the same quality, and afford the opportunity to take the same or equivalent courses of study;

b. The establishment or maintenance, for religious or linguistic reasons, of separate educational systems or institutions offering an education which is in keeping with the wishes of the pupil's parents or legal guardians, if participation in such systems or attendance at such institutions is optional and if the education provided conforms to such standards as may be laid down or approved by the competent authorities, in particular for education of the same level;

c. The establishment or maintenance of private educational institutions, if the object of the institutions is not to secure the exclusion of any group but to provide educational facilities in addition to those provided by the public authorities, if the institutions are conducted in accordance with that object, and if the education provided conforms with such standards as may be laid down or approved by the competent authorities, in particular for education of the same level.

Article 3

In order to eliminate and prevent discrimination within the meaning of this Convention, the States Parties thereto undertake:

a. To abrogate any statutory provisions and any administrative instructions and to discontinue any administrative practices which involve discrimination in education;

b. To ensure, by legislation where necessary, that there is no discrimination in the admission of pupils to educational institutions;

c. Not to allow any differences of treatment by the public authorities between nationals, except on the basis of merit or need, in the matter of school fees and the grant of scholarships or other forms of assistance to pupils and necessary permits and facilities for the pursuit of studies in foreign countries;

d. Not to allow, in any form of assistance granted by the public authorities to educational institutions, any restrictions or preference based solely on the ground that pupils belong to a particular group;

e. To give foreign nationals resident within their territory the same access to education as that given to their own nationals.

Article 4

The States Parties to this Convention undertake furthermore to formulate, develop and apply a national policy which, by methods appropriate to the circumstances and to national usage, will tend to promote equality of opportunity and of treatment in the matter of education and in particular:

a. To make primary education free and compulsory; make secondary education in its different forms generally available and accessible to all; make higher education equally accessible to all on the basis of individual capacity; assure compliance by all with the obligation to attend school prescribed by law;

b. To ensure that the standards of education are equivalent in all public education institutions of the same level, and that the conditions relating to the quality of education provided are also equivalent;

c. To encourage and intensify by appropriate methods the education of persons who have not received any primary education or who have not completed the entire primary education course and the continuation of their education on the basis of individual capacity;

d. To provide training for the teaching profession without discrimination.

Article 5

1. The States Parties to this Convention agree that:

a. Education shall be directed to the full development of the human personality and to the strengthening of respect for human rights and fundamental freedoms; it shall promote understanding, tolerance and friendship among all nations, racial or religious groups, and shall further the activities of the United Nations for the maintenance of peace;

b. It is essential to respect the liberty of parents and, where applicable, of legal guardians, firstly to choose for their children institutions other than those maintained by the public authorities but conforming to such minimum educational standards as may be laid down or approved by the competent authorities and, secondly, to ensure in a manner consistent with the procedures followed in the State for the application of its legislation, the religious and moral education of the children in conformity with their own convictions; and no person or group of persons should be compelled to receive religious instruction inconsistent with his or their conviction;

c. It is essential to recognize the right of members of national minorities to carry on their own educational activities, including the maintenance of schools and, depending on the educational policy of each State, the use or the teaching of their own language, provided however:

i. That this right is not exercised in a manner which prevents the members of these minorities from understanding the culture and language of the community as a whole and from participating in its activities, or which prejudices national sovereignty;

ii. That the standard of education is not lower than the general standard laid down or approved by the competent authorities; and

iii. That attendance at such schools is optional.

2. The States Parties to this Convention undertake to take all necessary measures to ensure the application of the principles enunciated in paragraph 1 of this article.

Article 6

In the application of this Convention, the States Parties to it undertake to pay the greatest attention to any recommendations hereafter adopted by the General Conference of the United Nations Educational, Scientific and Cultural Organization defining the measures to be taken against the different forms of discrimination in education and for the purpose of ensuring equality of opportunity and treatment in education.

Article 7

The States Parties to this Convention shall in their periodic reports submitted to the General Conference of the United Nations Educational, Scientific and Cultural Organization on dates and in a manner to be determined by it, give information on the legislative and administrative provisions which they have adopted and other action which they have taken for the application of this Convention, including that taken for the formulation and the development of the national policy defined in article 4 as well as the results achieved and the obstacles encountered in the application of that policy.

Article 8

Any dispute which may arise between any two or more States Parties to this Convention concerning the interpretation or application of this Convention which is not settled by negotiations shall at the request of the Parties to the dispute be referred, failing other means of settling the dispute, to the International Court of Justice for decision.

Article 9

Reservations to this Convention shall not be permitted.

Article 10

This Convention shall not have the effect of diminishing the rights which individuals or groups may enjoy by virtue of agreements concluded between two or more States, where such rights are not contrary to the letter or spirit of this Convention.

Article 11

This Convention is drawn up in English, French, Russian and Spanish, the four texts being equally authoritative.

Article 12

1. This Convention shall be subject to ratification or acceptance by States Members of the United Nations Educational, Scientific and Cultural Organization in accordance with their respective constitutional procedures.

2. The instruments of ratification or acceptance shall be deposited with the Director-General of the United Nations Educational, Scientific and Cultural Organization.

Article 13

1. This Convention shall be open to accession by all States not Members of the United Nations Educational, Scientific and Cultural Organization which are invited to do so by the Executive Board of the Organization.

2. Accession shall be effected by the deposit of an instrument of accession with the Director-General of the United Nations Educational, Scientific and Cultural Organization.

Article 14

This Convention shall enter into force three months after the date of the deposit of the third instrument of ratification, acceptance or accession, but only with respect to those States which have deposited their respective instruments on or before that date. It shall enter into force with respect to any other State three months after the deposit of its instrument of ratification, acceptance or accession.

Article 15

The States Parties to this Convention recognize that the Convention is applicable not only to their metropolitan territory but also to all non-self-governing, trust, colonial and other territories for the international relations of which they are responsible; they undertake to consult, if necessary, the governments or other competent authorities of these territories on or before ratification, acceptance or accession with a view to securing the application of the Convention to those territories, and to notify the Director-General of the United Nations Educational, Scientific and Cultural Organization of the territories to which it is accordingly applied, the notification to take effect three months after the date of its receipt.

Article 16

1. Each State Party to this Convention may denounce the Convention on its own behalf or on behalf of any territory for whose international relations it is responsible.

2. The denunciation shall be notified by an instrument in writing, deposited with the Director-General of the United Nations Educational, Scientific and Cultural Organization.

3. The denunciation shall take effect twelve months after the receipt of the instrument of denunciation.

Article 17

The Director-General of the United Nations Educational, Scientific and Cultural Organization shall inform the States Members of the Organization, the States not members of the Organization which are referred to in article 13, as well as the United Nations, of the deposit of all the instruments of ratification, acceptance and accession provided for in articles 12 and 13, and of notifications and denunciations provided for in articles 15 and 16 respectively.

Article 18

1. This Convention may be revised by the General Conference of the United Nations Educational, Scientific and Cultural Organization. Any such revision shall, however, bind only the States which shall become Parties to the revising convention.

2. If the General Conference should adopt a new convention revising this Convention in whole or in part, then, unless the new convention otherwise provides, this Convention shall cease to be open to ratification, acceptance or accession as from the date on which the new revising convention enters into force.

Article 19

In conformity with Article 102 of the Charter of the United Nations, this Convention shall be registered with the Secretariat of the United Nations at the request of the Director-General of the United Nations Educational, Scientific and Cultural Organization.

DONE in Paris, this fifteenth day of December 1960, in two authentic copies bearing the signatures of the President of the eleventh session of the General Conference and of the Director-General of the United Nations Educational, Scientific and Cultural Organization, which shall be deposited in the archives of the United Nations Educational, Scientific and Cultural Organization, and certified true copies of which shall be delivered to all the States referred to in articles 12 and 13 as well as to the United Nations.

The foregoing is the authentic text of the Convention duly adopted by the General Conference of the United Nations Educational, Scientific and Cultural Organization during its eleventh session, which was held in Paris and declared closed the fifteenth day of December 1960.

IN FAITH WHEREOF we have appended our signatures this fifteenth day of December 1960.

Appendix 2

Education Agenda of the International Community: Education 2030

Incheon Declaration: Towards inclusive and equitable quality education and lifelong learning for all

Framework for Action (extracts) 2015[183]

A United Nations Summit meeting in New York from 25 to 27 September 2015, as the Organisation celebrated its 70th anniversary, adopted the Resolution "Transforming our World: The 2030 Agenda for Sustainable Development" (A/RES/70/1), with 17 Sustainable Development Goals (SDGs) and 169 targets, to be reached by 2030. *Goal 4* reads as follows: *Ensure inclusive and equitable quality education and promote lifelong learning opportunities for all.* It unfolds in 10 sub-goals.

In the context of the preparation of the 2030 Agenda for Sustainable Development, UNESCO together with UNICEF, the World Bank and other international entities organised a World Education Forum in Incheon, Republic of Korea, from 19 to 22 May 2015, with about 1600 participants from 160 countries, including 120 Ministers. It was prepared by, among other initiatives, a Global Thematic Consultation on Education in the Post-2015 Development Agenda, co-led by UNESCO and UNICEF (2013) and the already mentioned UNESCO Report *Rethinking education* (2015).

The Incheon World Education Forum adopted the Incheon Declaration. On 4 November, an Education 2030 Framework for Action for the Implementation of Sustainable Development Goal 4 was adopted by 184 UNESCO's Member States, in Paris, and endorsed by the General Conference. The Incheon Declaration and the Education 2030 Framework for Action represent, therefore, the medium-term commitments of the International Community towards the right to education.

The most significant feature of the 2030 Agenda for Sustainable Development is that it takes an overtly human rights approach (there are 14 references to them). So do the Incheon Declaration and the Education 2030 Framework for Action. Other of their most important features include:

- They address both developing and developed countries.

- Not losing sight of the hundreds of million children and adolescents still out of school, and of the illiterate persons, the main focus is now on education quality.

- At least one year of free and compulsory quality pre-primary education should be available, and free school education should cover 12 years, 9 of which compulsory.

- The principle of lifelong education is adopted.

Incheon Declaration: Towards inclusive and equitable quality education and lifelong learning for all

Preamble

1. We, Ministers, heads and members of delegations, heads of agencies and officials of multilateral and bilateral organizations, and representatives of civil society, the teaching profession, youth and the private sector, have gathered in May 2015 at the invitation of the Director-General of UNESCO in Incheon, Republic of Korea, for the World Education Forum 2015 (WEF 2015). […]

2. On this historic occasion, we reaffirm the vision of the worldwide movement for Education for All initiated in Jomtien in 1990 and reiterated in Dakar in 2000 – the most important commitment to education in recent decades and which has helped drive significant progress in education. We also reaffirm the vision and political will reflected in numerous international and regional human rights treaties that stipulate the right to education and its interrelation with other human rights. We acknowledge the efforts made; however, we recognize with great concern that we are far from having reached education for all.

…

4. Having taken stock of progress made towards the EFA goals since 2000 and the education-related Millennium Development Goals (MDGs) as well as the lessons learned, and having examined the remaining challenges and deliberated on the proposed Education 2030 agenda and the Framework for Action as well as on future priorities and strategies for its achievement, we adopt this Declaration.

Towards 2030: a new vision for education

5. Our vision […] is inspired by a humanistic vision of education and development based on human rights and dignity; social justice; inclusion; protection; cultural, linguistic and ethnic diversity; and shared responsibility and accountability. We reaffirm that education is a public good, a fundamental human right and a basis for guaranteeing the realization of other rights. […]

6. Motivated by our significant achievements in expanding access to education over the last 15 years, we will ensure the provision of 12 years of free, publicly funded, equitable quality primary and secondary education, of which at least nine years are compulsory, leading to relevant learning outcomes. We also encourage the provision of at least one year of free and compulsory quality pre-primary education and that all children have access to quality early childhood development, care and education. We also commit to providing meaningful education and training opportunities for the large population of out-of-school children and adolescents, who require immediate, targeted and sustained action ensuring that all children are in school and are learning.

...

14. ... We therefore are determined to increase public spending on education in accordance with country context, and urge adherence to the international and regional benchmarks of allocating efficiently at least 4 – 6% of Gross Domestic Product and/or at least 15 – 20% of total public expenditure to education.

15. ... We recognize that the fulfilment of all commitments related to official development assistance (ODA) is crucial, including the commitments by many developed countries to achieve the target of 0.7 per cent of gross national product (GNP) for ODA to developing countries. [...]

Framework for Action

Introduction

1. The world has made some remarkable progress in education since 2000, when the six Education for All (EFA) goals and the Millennium Development Goals (MDGs) were established. Those goals were not, however, reached by the 2015 deadline and continued action is needed to complete the unfinished agenda. With Goal 4 of *Transforming our world: the 2030 Agenda for Sustainable Development – 'Ensure inclusive and equitable quality education and promote lifelong learning opportunities for all'* (hereafter referred to as *SDG4-Education* 2030) – and its associated targets, the world has set a more ambitious universal education agenda for the period from 2015 to 2030. Every effort must be made to guarantee that this time the goal and targets are achieved.

2. SDG4-Education 2030 was developed through a broad consultative process [...]. This process culminated in the Incheon Declaration, which was adopted on 21 May 2015 at the World Education Forum (WEF 2015) held in Incheon, Republic of Korea. The Incheon Declaration constitutes the commitment of the education community to SDG4-Education 2030 and the 2030 Agenda for Sustainable Development. [...]

...

I. *Vision, rationale and principles*

...

10. The principles informing this Framework are drawn from international instruments and agreements [...]. Those principles include:

- *Education is a fundamental human right and an enabling right.* [...] Education shall aim at the full development of the human personality and promote mutual understanding, tolerance, friendship and peace.

- *Education is a public good* [...]. The role of the State is essential in setting and regulating standards and norms.

- *Gender equality is inextricably linked to the right to education for all.* [...]

Appendix 3
Revisiting a classical question: How to solve the Gordian Knot of education?

The educational phenomenon is a process of cultural and social integration of the coming generations, so that the new members of each community become *good* and *useful,* according to common values and needs. Underlying, is a representation of *human nature* and a vision of *good education.*

In light of the best present knowledge, the human nature is dual, as we saw: it is inextricably biological (innate) and cultural (acquired):

- The biological nature is the objective substratum of the human perfectibility or educability, that is, of the possibility and need of perfecting human beings, through education.

- The cultural nature results from education as a formal, non-formal and informal phenomenon of multiple influences and experiences, throughout life, and as a collective, politically oriented interest.

Therefore, education cannot be thought of and improved in isolation, as if it were not a culturally and socially embedded phenomenon. Nor can a society be thought of and improved without considering the educational phenomenon as the cradle of reproduction of the material and mental conditions of its existence. Education and politics are Siamese sisters, interconnected by an umbilical cord that cannot be ignored without risk of falling into a sterile, possibly violent, voluntarism.

This symbiosis is one of the reasons why politics and education have been frequently considered not only as the main arts but also the most difficult ones, even "impossible" (Aristotle, Comenius, Locke, Rousseau, Kant, Freud). In effect, both political theorisation and pedagogical theorisation end up confronting a *Gordian Knot*[184]. Great thinkers, at least since Plato and his *Republic,* were confronted with it.

The *political Gordian Knot* is about the control of political power. The less bad solution, so far, is the Rule of Law, with its checks and balances, and democracy as a political regime in which citizens can elect their rulers, directly or indirectly. They are supposed to elect the best ones to govern for the Common Good, but they can be deceived, misled and lose control of the exercise of a power so decisive for their lives.

The *pedagogical Gordian Knot* is about the education of educators. The professionalisation of school education has improved the effectiveness of instruction, but little so education as a global process of the human personality formation. And mothers and fathers – who are in fact the first education 'professionals' – generally do not learn how to educate their children. It is assumed that progenitors are naturally good (if not the best) educators.

If education is ultimately politically decided by rulers whose education necessarily influences their decisions, the political Gordian Knot has a pedagogical dimension, and the pedagogical Gordian Knot has a political dimension, chained in a vicious circle of reproduction of so many human ills.

How to break it?

The human species must govern and educate itself – this is its inescapable reality and destiny. Therefore, it has no choice but to make the circle of the political-pedagogical Gordian Knot less vicious and more virtuous.

Where to start?

The brief preamble of the 1924 Geneva Declaration of the Rights of the Child[185] proclaimed that "mankind owes to the child the best it has to give" (in French: *l'humanité se doit de donner à l'enfant le meilleur d'elle-*

même; in Spanish: *la humanidad debe dar al niño lo mejor que puede darle*). These words have been taken up in the last paragraph of the Preamble of the 1959 Declaration of the Rights of the Child. They were kept in the first project for a Convention on the Rights of the Child presented by Poland to the UN Commission on Human Rights, in 1978, but have been left out in the final text adopted in 1989. Unfortunately, because they are probably the most sublime words of International Human Rights Law.

Considering that education is humanly primordial – especially first education and moral education – this may be the *Principle* of dissolution of the political-pedagogical Gordian Knot: it will begin to be decisively dissolved when the right to education be *right of children to learn to be human with the best human beings*, that is, with educators who personify *the best* of Humanity.

What is *the best* of Humanity?

The best of the humankind is not its level of material well-being, which can be destroyed by the insanity and barbarity of never ceasing wars. Nor its powerful science and prodigious technology, which may be used to mistreat, torture and kill. Not even the great artistic creations of the species' *divine* genius, which its demonic genius can pulverise. What can save the humankind from itself is the Ethics of Human Rights as the quintessence of its conscience and ideal of its becoming. Being so, *the best* the humankind has to give to every child, at present, is the Convention on the Rights of the Child as the fairy of their destiny...

The child's human right to education is potentially a dissolver of the political-pedagogical Gordian Knot.

The circle of the pedagogical-political Gordian Knot will become increasing less vicious and more virtuous as education be *scientifically* grounded in the most advanced knowledge of human nature, *ethically* enlightened by the highest vision of human perfection and *politically* entrusted to the best human beings by better rulers, elected by better educated citizens, better educators of their children.

There is no realistic and humanistic alternative to *the best* for educating and governing.

Notes

[1] https://digitallibrary.un.org/record/1487535
[2] https://digitallibrary.un.org/record/432638
[3] http://www.un.org/en/sections/un-charter/un-charter-full-text/
[4] https://www.europarl.europa.eu/charter/pdf/text_en.pdf
[5]https://undocs.org/Home/Mobile?FinalSymbol=A%2FRES%2F41%2F120&Language=E&DeviceType=Desktop&LangRequested=False
[6] https://www.un.org/en/about-us/un-charter/full-text
[7] https://www.un.org/en/about-us/un-charter/full-text
[8]https://tbinternet.ohchr.org/_layouts/15/treatybodyexternal/Download.aspx?symbolno=CCPR%2FC%2F21%2FRev.1%2FAdd.13&Lang=en
[9] *Jurisprudence,* in the ancient sense, is synonym with Philosophy of Law or Science of Law. In the modern sense, as distinguished from Case Law (claims brought before Tribunals or Courts), it means the judicial interpretation of rules and decisions (for example, the jurisprudence on the right to education).
Doctrine, a term whose Latin etymology is *docere* (to teach), denotes the opinions and comments on legal issues, published in treatises, textbooks, articles, chronicles, theses, monographs, etc. It also includes Advisory Opinions of International Courts, as well as interpretations of legal norms by other established bodies. By influencing Legislators and Judges, the Doctrine also participates in the creation, interpretation and evolution of the Law.
[10] https://www.icj-cij.org/en/statute
[11] Numbers on June 2023: https://indicators.ohchr.org/
[12] https://eur-lex.europa.eu/legal-content/EN/TXT/?uri=CELEX:12007L/TXT
It should be noted that, according to Article 6.2 of the Treaty of Lisbon: "The Union shall accede to the European Convention for the Protection of Human Rights and Fundamental Freedoms." On its turn, Article 59.2 of the European Convention, as amended by its Protocol 14, provides: "The European Union may accede to this Convention." The negotiating process is not yet completed.
(https://www.echr.coe.int/documents/d/echr/Convention_ENG)
[13] Composed of the majority of the Republics comprising the former USSR (Union of Soviet Socialist Republics). (https://www.refworld.org/docid/49997ae32c.html)
[14] https://www.ohchr.org/en/what-are-human-rights/international-bill-human-rights
[15] https://legal.un.org/ilc/texts/instruments/english/conventions/1_1_1969.pdf
[16]https://undocs.org/Home/Mobile?FinalSymbol=CRC%2FC%2F90&Language=E&DeviceType=Desktop&LangRequested=False
[17]https://tbinternet.ohchr.org/_layouts/15/treatybodyexternal/Download.aspx?symbolno=CCPR%2FC%2F21%2FRev.1%2FAdd.13&Lang=en
[18] https://www.fidh.org/IMG/pdf/maastricht-eto-principles-uk_web.pdf
The Maastricht Principles were adopted on 28 September 2011 by 40 International Law experts from around the world, after more than a decade of research, at a gathering

convened by the International Commission of Jurists (Genf, Switzerland), the Faculty of Law of the University of Limburg (Maastricht, Netherlands), and the Urban Morgan Institute for Human Rights, University of Cincinnati College of Law (Ohio, USA). The Maastricht Principles complement and build on the Limburg Principles (1986) and on the Maastricht Guidelines (1997).

The *Limburg Principles on the Implementation of the International Covenant on Economic, Social and Cultural Rights* were approved by a group of 29 experts in International Law meeting in Maastricht on 2-6 June 1986, convened by the same entities, for considering especially the nature and scope of the obligations of States Parties to the 1966 International Covenant, when the respective Committee was established.
(https://hlrn.org/img/documents/Limburg%20Principles.pdf)

The *Maastricht Guidelines on Violations of Economic, Social and Cultural Rights* were adopted by more than 30 experts on International Law meeting in Maastricht on 22-26 January 1997, convened by the same institutions for debating the violations of the economic, social and cultural rights, and the measures to be taken as well.
(https://www.refworld.org/docid/48abd5730.html)

[19]https://tbinternet.ohchr.org/_layouts/15/treatybodyexternal/Download.aspx?symbolno=CCPR%2FC%2F21%2FRev.1%2FAdd.13&Lang=en

[20] https://www.refworld.org/docid/4538838e10.html

[21] For example, the German Constitution (Article 19.2) states: "In no case may the essence of a basic right be affected." (https://www.gesetze-im-internet.de/gg/index.html)

[22] https://www.ohchr.org/en/about-us/history/vienna-declaration

[23] https://www.un.org/en/genocideprevention/about-responsibility-to-protect.shtml

[24] The Constitution of the Republic of South Africa (1996) states (8.2): "A provision of the Bill of Rights binds a natural or a juristic person if, and to the extent that, it is applicable, taking into account the nature of the right and the nature of any duty imposed by the right."
(https://justice.gov.za/legislation/constitution/SAConstitution-web-eng-0.pdf)

[25] In 2019, the UN International Law Commission completed a Draft Convention on the Prohibition and Punishment of Crimes Against Humanity, not yet adopted. (https://legal.un.org/ilc/guide/7_7.shtml)

[26] https://www.ohchr.org/en/about-us/history/vienna-declaration

[27] *Rule of Law* is a term that does not translate the full content of the German concept *Rechtsstaat*, as does the French *État de Droit*.

[28] https://www.ohchr.org/en/instruments-mechanisms/instruments/principles-relating-status-national-institutions-paris#:~:text=Principles%20relating%20to%20the%20Status%20of%20National%20Institutions,with%20competence%20to%20promote%20and%20protect%20human%20rights.

[29] In Colombia, *Acción de Tutela* (Protection Action) is a summary recourse before any Judge (laid down in Article 86 of the Constitution), to achieve a quick and effective decision (the Judge has 10 days to decide), without prejudice to the minimum formalities required by the basic principle of due process. It can be filed even by a child and admits appeal to the Constitutional Court. It is the so-called "Liberty Jurisdiction", already used by millions of citizens.
(https://www.corteconstitucional.gov.co/lacorte/DECRETO%202591.php)

[30]https://www.eui.eu/Documents/DepartmentsCentres/AcademyofEuropeanLaw/CourseMaterialsHR/HR2009/Scheinin/ScheininClassReading2.pdf
[31] That means the supremacy of human dignity over State's authority, quite the opposite of the Nazi slogan: "You are nothing, your volk is everything" (*Du bist nichts, dein Volk ist alles*). The German Federal Constitutional Court said (*BVerfG, 2 BvB 1/13,* 17 January 2017, para. 540):

> The absolute subjugation of a person to a collective, an ideology or a religion amounts to a violation of the value accorded to all human beings for their own sake simply by virtue of their being persons (BVerfGE 115, 118). It violates the individual's quality as a subject and constitutes an interference with the guarantee of human dignity which fundamentally violates the free democratic basic order.

(https://www.bundesverfassungsgericht.de/SharedDocs/Entscheidungen/EN/2017/01/bs20170117_2bvb000113en.html#:~:text=-%202%20BvB%201%2F13%20-%201.%20The%20prohibition,rule%20of%20law%20has%20against%20an%20organised%20enemy)

[32] According to the Draft Outline of an International Bill of Human Rights prepared by the Division of Human Rights of the United Nations Secretariat in 1947 (E/CN.4/ AC.1/3), one of the four principles its Preamble should enunciate was: "that man is a citizen both of his State and of the world".
(https://documents-dds-ny.un.org/doc/UNDOC/GEN/NG9/000/25/PDF/NG900025.pdf?OpenElement)
[33] https://www.echr.coe.int/documents/d/echr/convention_ENG
[34]https://hudoc.echr.coe.int/eng#{%22fulltext%22:[%22https://www.globalhealthrights.org/wp-content/uploads/2013/02/ECtHR-2003-Van-Kuck-v-Germany.pdf%22],%22documentcollectionid2%22:[%22GRANDCHAMBER%22,%22CHAMBER%22],%22itemid%22:[%22001-61142%22]}
[35] The *Grundgesetz* (Basic Law) was so called, because it was not a Constitution democratically legitimised, but was drafted by a Parliamentary Council, following the Frankfurt Documents issued from a Conference held in London in 1948, gathering the Western powers and Belgium, Netherlands and Luxembourg. According to its original Article 146: "This Basic Law shall become invalid on the day a Constitution freely adopted by the German people takes effect." However, after the German reunification (1989/1990), it was eventually considered that no referendum was needed and the *Grundgesetz* should remain in force.
[36] https://www.gesetze-im-internet.de/gg/index.html
Although "intangible" is the most literal translation, the most frequent is "inviolable".
[37] https://www.europarl.europa.eu/charter/pdf/text_en.pdf
[38] The German Federal Constitutional Court remarked (*BVerfGE 39, 1,* 25 February 1975, para. 109):

> The express incorporation into the Basic Law of the self-evident right to life – in contrast to the Weimar Constitution – may be explained principally as a reaction to the "destruction of life unworthy of life," to the "final solution" and "liquidations,"

which were carried out by the National Socialistic Regime as measures of State.

(https://groups.csail.mit.edu/mac/users/rauch/germandecision/german_abortion_decision2.html)

The Constitutional Court of South Africa said in *Prinsloo v. Van Der Linde and Another* (Case CCT 4/96, 18 April 1997):

> (31) … We are emerging from a period of our history during which the humanity of the majority of the inhabitants of this country was denied. They were treated as not having inherent worth; as objects whose identities could be arbitrarily defined by those in power rather than as persons of infinite worth […]. In short, they were denied recognition of their inherent dignity.

(http://www.saflii.org/za/cases/ZACC/1997/5.html)

And in *Dawood and Another v Minister of Home Affairs and Others* (Case CCT 35/99, 7 June 2000):

> (35) The value of dignity in our Constitutional framework cannot therefore be doubted. The Constitution asserts dignity to contradict our past in which human dignity for black South Africans was routinely and cruelly denied. It asserts it too to inform the future, to invest in our democracy respect for the intrinsic worth of all human beings.

(http://www.saflii.org/za/cases/ZACC/2000/8.html)

[39] The Constitution of the Portuguese Republic (1974) is also considered a reference. It mentions "dignity" six times and devotes its Part I to "Fundamental Rights and Duties", with dozens of long provisions (Articles 12 to 79), being probably the longest human rights catalogue in Constitutional Law.
(https://www.parlamento.pt/sites/EN/Parliament/Documents/Constitution7th.pdf)
[40] The so-called "eternity clause" laid down in Article 79.3 of the German Basic Law commands that amendments, *inter alia,* of its Articles 1 to 20 ("Basic Rights" and "Constitutional Principles") "shall be inadmissible".
The South Africa Constitution provides (74.1.2) that Chapter 2 (Bill of Rights):

> … may be amended by a Bill passed by:
> (a) the National Assembly, with a supporting vote of at least two thirds of its members; and
> (b) the National Council of Provinces, with a supporting vote of at least six provinces.

[41]https://www.bundesverfassungsgericht.de/SharedDocs/Entscheidungen/EN/2006/02/rs20060215_1bvr035705en.html

The acronym 'BVerfGE' means 'Federal Constitutional Court Decisions', the following numbers indicating the volume and first page where the Decision was officially published.
The German Federal Constitutional Court is composed of two *Senates* (Senates), each consisting of eight Justices (which may meet in Plenary), each Senate forming three Chambers (*Kammern*).
[42] Adopted in 1996 and entered into force on 4 February 1996, replacing an Interim Constitution that had come into effect on 27 April 1994.
(www.parliament.gov.za/storage/app/media/Acts/constitution/SAConstitution.pdf)
[43]https://undocs.org/Home/Mobile?FinalSymbol=A%2FC.3%2FSR.99&Language=E&DeviceType=Desktop&LangRequested=False
[44] *Floating Signifier* is an expression (originated from Claude Lévi-Strauss) denoting a signifier without a referent determined. Therefore, it may be used with different arguments.
[45] South African Constitution states (10): "Everyone has inherent dignity and the right to have their dignity respected and protected." Commenting on this provision, the Constitutional Court said in *Dawood and Another v Minister of Home Affairs and Others* (Case CCT 35/99, 7 June 2000) that human dignity:

> (35) … is a value that informs the interpretation of many, possibly all, other rights. […] Section 10, however, makes it plain that dignity is not only a value fundamental to our Constitution; it is a justiciable and enforceable right that must be respected and protected. In many cases, however, where the value of human dignity is offended, the primary constitutional breach occasioned may be of a more specific right […].

(http://www.saflii.org/za/cases/ZACC/2000/8.html)
[46] Nevertheless, a distinction can be made between human dignity and human rights, pointed out by the European Court of Human Rights in *Case of Vo v. France* (Application 53924/00, 8 July 2004). It said: While "there is no consensus on the nature and status of the embryo and/or foetus (see paragraphs 39–40 above)", it is recognised "that the embryo/foetus belongs to the human race. The potentiality of that being and its capacity to become a person […] require protection in the name of human dignity, without making it a 'person' with the 'right to life' for the purposes of Article 2" (para. 84).
(https://hudoc.echr.coe.int/eng?i=001-61887#{%22itemid%22:[%22001-61887%22]})

[47] https://undocs.org/E/C.12/1999/10
[48] www.ohchr.org/en/professionalinterest/pages/vienna.aspx
[49] https://archive.org/details/TheLittlePrince-English
Original text: http://gutenberg.net.au/ebooks03/0300771h.html
[50]http://portal.unesco.org/en/ev.php-URL_ID=13177&URL_DO=DO_TOPIC&URL_SECTION=201.html
[51] https://www.servat.unibe.ch/dfr/bv039001.html
[52] The German Federal Constitutional Court said (*BVerfGE 109, 279*, para. 116):

> The Federal Constitutional Court has repeatedly emphasized that it is incompatible with human dignity to make human beings mere objects of governmental power (see BVerfGE 30, 1 [25-26 and 39 et seq.]; 96, 375 [399]). For example, criminals may not be treated in a manner that violates their constitutionally protected right to social esteem and respect and thereby reduced to mere objects of crime prevention and prosecution (see BVerfGE 45, 187 [228]; 72, 105 [116]).

(https://www.servat.unibe.ch/dfr/bv109279.html)

[53] For example, Justice Ackermann, ruling as member of the Constitutional Court of South Africa, said in *Ferreira v Levin NO and Others* (CCT 5/95, 6 December 1995, para. 52):

> Kant luminously conceptualises freedom as the "only one innate right" in the following terms:
>
> "Freedom (independence from the constraint of another's will), insofar as it is compatible with the freedom of everyone else in accordance with a universal law, is the one sole and original right that belongs to every human being by virtue of his humanity."

(http://www.saflii.org/za/cases/ZACC/1995/13.html)

The South African Constitution is also influenced by the African idea of *uBuntu*, following which the human beings are human together and should, therefore, recognise and respect each other.

[54] According to Article 20 (Constitutional principles – Right of resistance) of the German Constitution: "The Federal Republic of Germany is a democratic and social federal State." (para. 1) And Article 28 (Land constitutions – Autonomy of municipalities] refers to "the principles of a republican, democratic and social State governed by the rule of law [*Rechtsstaat*] within the meaning of this Basic Law" (para. 1).
(https://www.gesetze-im-internet.de/gg/index.html)

The social principle was given statutory force in the German General Social Code (*Sozialgesetzbuch*, SGB XII, § 1), according to which: "It is the objective of social aid [*Sozialhilfe*] to enable those entitled to it to lead their lives in a manner which is consistent with human dignity."
(https://www.sozialgesetzbuch-sgb.de/sgbxii/1.html)

The South African Constitution mirrors the International Covenant on Social, Economic and Cultural Rights. Its Constitutional Court said in *Government of the Republic of South Africa and Others v. Grootboom and Others* (Case CCT 11/00, 4 October 2000, para. 23): "Our Constitution entrenches both civil and political rights and social and economic rights. All the rights in our Bill of Rights are inter-related and mutually supporting. There can be no doubt that human dignity, freedom and equality, the foundational values of our society, are denied those who have no food, clothing or shelter."
(http://www.saflii.org/za/cases/ZACC/2000/19.html)

---

[55] The Canadian Supreme Court said in *Law v. Canada (Minister of Employment and Immigration)*: "What is human dignity? There can be different conceptions of what human dignity means. […] It is concerned with physical and psychological integrity and empowerment." (para. 53)
(https://scc-csc.lexum.com/scc-csc/scc-csc/en/item/1691/index.do)
[56] The German Federal Constitutional Court said (2 *BvB 1/13*, 17 January 2017, para. 538):

> The free democratic basic order is rooted primarily in human dignity (Art. 1(1) GG). This is recognised in the case-law of the Federal Constitutional Court as the highest value of the Basic Law (cf. BVerfGE 5, 85 <204>; 12, 45 <53>; 27, 1 <6>; 35, 202 <225>; 45, 187 <227>; 87, 209 <228>; 96, 375 <399>). Human dignity is not subject to disposition. The State must respect and protect it in all its forms (cf. BVerfGE 45, 187 <227>). This deprives the State and its legal system of any absoluteness and any "natural" precedence.

(https://www.bverfg.de/e/bs20170117_2bvb000113en.html)

[57] The German Federal Constitutional Court said (*BVerfGE 115, 118*, para. 119):

> All human beings possess this dignity as persons, irrespective of their qualities, their physical or mental state, their achievements and their social status (see BVerfGE 87, 209 [228]; 96, 375 [399]). It cannot be taken away from any human being. What can be violated, however, is the claim to respect which results from it (see BVerfGE 87, 209 [228]).

(https://www.bundesverfassungsgericht.de/SharedDocs/Entscheidungen/DE/2006/02/rs20060215_1bvr035705.html)

[58] The Constitutional Court of South Africa said in *Khumalo and Others v. Holomisa* (Case CCT 53/01, 14 June 2002, para. 27):

> The value of human dignity in our Constitution […] includes the intrinsic worth of human beings shared by all people as well as the individual reputation of each person built upon his or her own individual achievements. The value of human dignity in our Constitution therefore values both the personal sense of self-worth as well as the public's estimation of the worth or value of an individual.

(http://www.saflii.org/za/cases/ZACC/2002/12.html)

[59] For example, in the opinion of the Canadian Supreme Court in *R v. Keegstra* (Report [1990] 3 SCR 697, 13 December 1990): "A person's sense of human dignity and belonging to a community is closely linked to the concern and respect accorded the groups to which he or she belongs. The derision, hostility and abuse encouraged by hate propaganda therefore have a severe impact on the individual's sense of self-worth and acceptance."
(https://scc-csc.lexum.com/scc-csc/scc-csc/en/item/695/index.do)
The Constitutional Court of South Africa observed in *S v. Williams and Others* (CCT20/94,

9 June 1995, para. 47): "If the State, as role model *par excellence*, treats the weakest and the most vulnerable among us in a manner that diminishes rather than enhances their self-esteem and human dignity, the danger increases that their regard for a culture of decency and respect for the rights of others will be diminished."
(http://www.saflii.org/za/cases/ZACC/1995/6.html)

[60] The same Constitutional Court said in *Khosa and Others v Minister of Social Development and Others* (Case CCT 12/03, 4 March 2004): "Sharing responsibility for the problems and consequences of poverty equally as a community represents the extent to which wealthier members of the community view the minimal well-being of the poor as connected with their personal well-being and the well-being of the community as a whole." (para. 74) (http://www.saflii.org/za/cases/ZACC/2004/11.html)

[61] The dignity of deceased human beings survives physically in the genetic heritage they have transmitted to their children, affectively in the memory of their most beloved, symbolically in their names. They may also be immortalised by nations for the greatness of their creations or actions, to say nothing of faith in immortality. Other aspects of moral survival include the authors' rights (copyright), as well as the online profiles and data (digital remains). The German Federal Constitutional Court, while emphasising "that human dignity is distinct from the general right of personality", said (1 BvR 19/22, I.1): "It would be incompatible with the constitutional guarantee of the inviolability of human dignity, which is the root of all fundamental rights and applies to all human beings, if a person could be degraded or humiliated after their death in a manner affecting their general right to respect for their person (*Achtungsanspruch*)."
(https://www.bundesverfassungsgericht.de/SharedDocs/Pressemitteilungen/EN/2022/bvg22-108.html)

[62] https://supreme.justia.com/cases/federal/us/378/184/

[63] http://www.corteconstitucional.gov.co/relatoria/2016/t-363-16.htm

[64] Human life "is the living foundation of human dignity and the prerequisite for all other fundamental rights", as said the German Federal Constitutional Court (*BVerfGE 39, 1, 1975*, para. 124).
(https://www.servat.unibe.ch/dfr/bv039001.html)

[65] The Supreme Court of Israel said in *HCJ 6427/02 Movement for Quality Government in Israel v. Knesset,* quoted in *HCJ 2605/05 Academic Center of Law and Business v. Minister of Finance*[65] that "the essence of human dignity lies in the sanctity of his life and his liberty" (para. 34).
(http://www.antoniocasella.eu/nume/Israeli_HCJ_privatization_2009.pdf)

[66] English speakers can choose between 'liberty' and 'freedom' to express the same idea – a choice that no other European language offers. However, as there is no single agreed criterion to choose between them, they are generally considered interchangeable terms. If any useful distinction could be made, could one say that liberty is a more political and philosophical idea (the ideal of *liberté*), and freedom a more concrete concept (freedom to do this or that)?

[67] According to the German Federal Constitutional Court (*1 BvR 400/51*, 15 January 1958, para. 31): "The basic right to freedom of expression, the most immediate aspect of the human personality in society, is one of the most precious rights of man (Declaration of the Rights of Man and Citizen (1789) Article 11). It is absolutely essential to a free and democratic State […]. In a certain sense it is the basis of freedom itself […].

(https://www.bundesverfassungsgericht.de/SharedDocs/Downloads/DE/1958/01/rs195 80115_1bvr040051.pdf?__blob=publicationFile&v=1)
The South African Constitutional Court said in *Ferreira v Levin NO and Others* (CCT 5/95, 6 December 1995): "Without freedom, human dignity is little more than an abstraction. Freedom and dignity are inseparably linked. To deny people their freedom is to deny them their dignity."
(http://www.saflii.org/za/cases/ZACC/1995/13.html)
[68] https://unesdoc.unesco.org/ark:/48223/pf0000127160/PDF/127160por.pdf.multi
[69] The cruelty of the crimes of some serial killers may be motivated by the search for public notoriety. Some go so far as claiming to be credited with the authorship of crimes still under investigation…
[70] https://americanrhetoric.com/speeches/eleanorrooseveltdeclarationhumanrights.htm
[71] https://digitallibrary.un.org/record/701853?ln=en
[72] https://unesdoc.unesco.org/ark:/48223/pf0000386924?posInSet=1&queryId=88262d97-74b6-4100-bd33-8cc96a779989
[73] https://undocs.org/en/A/RES/63/116
[74] https://parliamentofreligions.org/wp-content/uploads/2023/05/Global-Ethic-PDF-2020-Update.pdf
[75] https://www.un.org/en/about-us/udhr/history-of-the-declaration
[76] "Democracy is more than a parliamentary form of government. It is a philosophy of life [*Weltanschauung*] based on the appreciation of the dignity, the value and the inalienable rights of each individual human being. A true democracy must respect these rights and the value of each and every human being in all respects of political, economic and cultural life." (Konrad Adenauer, Chairman of the Parliamentary Council that drafted the *Grundgesetz* who became the first German *Bundeskanzler* (Chancellor), 1949-1963.
(https://www.konrad-adenauer.de/zitate/demokratie/)
In a Case related to the prohibition of political parties (*BVerfG, 2 BvB 1/13,* 17 January 2017), the German Federal Constitutional Court said, mentioning "the historical experience of the rise of the Nazi party in the Weimar Republic" (para. 621): "The free democratic basic order is rooted primarily in human dignity (Art. 1(1) GG)." (3.a) Its "constituent elements" are "human dignity, democracy and the rule of law", which "are interlocked and mutually dependent" (para. 556) .
[77] https://www.archives.gov/founding-docs/declaration-transcript
[78] http://avalon.law.yale.edu/18th_century/rightsof.asp
[79] http://www.un.org/en/sections/un-charter/un-charter-full-text/
[80] This was so expressed by the German Federal Constitutional Court (*1 BvR 400/51, 15,* January 1958, para. 24-25):

> There is no doubt that the main purpose of basic rights is to protect the individual's sphere of freedom against encroachment by public power: they are the citizen's bulwark against the State […].
> But far from being a value-free system the Constitution erects an objective system of values in its section on basic rights, and thus expresses and reinforces the validity of the basic rights. This system of values, centring on the freedom of the human being to develop in society, must apply as a constitutional axiom throughout the

> whole legal system: it must direct and inform legislation, administration, and judicial decision. It naturally influences private law as well; no rule of private law may conflict with it, and all such rules must be construed in accordance with its spirit.

(https://www.bundesverfassungsgericht.de/SharedDocs/Downloads/DE/1958/01/rs19580115_1bvr040051.pdf?__blob=publicationFile&v=1)

[81] *Press Release SG/SM/6697 NGO/306 PI/1079 14 September 1998*: https://www.un.org/press/en/1998/19980914.sgsm6697.html
[82] http://ap.ohchr.org/documents/alldocs.aspx?doc_id=2880
[83]https://undocs.org/Home/Mobile?FinalSymbol=CRC%2FGC%2F2003%2F5&Language=E&DeviceType=Desktop&LangRequested=False
[84] https://undocs.org/A/RES/836(IX)
[85]https://undocs.org/Home/Mobile?FinalSymbol=CRC%2FGC%2F2001%2F1&Language=E&DeviceType=Desktop&LangRequested=False
[86] https://www.ohchr.org/en/instruments-mechanisms/instruments/convention-rights-child
[87] https://www2.ohchr.org/English/bodies/crc/docs/GC/CRC_C_GC_14_ENG.pdf
[88] A *serial killer* in the US testified in an interrogation: "My mother never said to me, *I love you...*
[89] http://www.un-documents.net/a14r1386.htm
[90] https://www.ohchr.org/en/professionalinterest/pages/crc.aspx
[91] www2.ohchr.org/english/bodies/crc/docs/AdvanceVersions/GeneralComment7Rev1.pdf
[92] https://digitallibrary.un.org/record/108125
[93]https://undocs.org/Home/Mobile?FinalSymbol=CRC/C/GC/8&Language=E&DeviceType=Desktop&LangRequested=False
[94] Also the German Federal Constitutional Court stressed the revolutionary meaning of the rights of the child when it said (*BVerfGE) 121, 69*, para. 71, 21 November 2007) that "the child is not the object of parental exercise of rights, it is a legal subject and holder of fundamental rights in whose best interest parents are obliged to act".
(https://www.servat.unibe.ch/dfr/bv121069.html)
[95]https://undocs.org/Home/Mobile?FinalSymbol=E%2FCN.4%2FAC.1%2F3%2FADD.1&Language=E&DeviceType=Desktop&LangRequested=False
[96] http://www.planalto.gov.br/ccivil_03/Constituicao/Constituicao34.htm
[97] Let us add, quoting a Special Rapporteur on the Right to Education (Kishore Singh, A/HRC/23/35):

> 25. The right to education is enshrined in the constitutions of a large number of countries – it is one of the most universally recognized rights in national constitutions in the world today. A study of national constitutions found that 90 per cent of constitutions in the world contain a provision on the right to education. Of those constitutions that contain education provisions, 56 per cent require that education be compulsory up to a certain level. Additionally, 65 per cent of these constitutions stipulate that education should be free up to a certain level. Moreover, national legislation on education exists in most States.

https://undocs.org/Home/Mobile?FinalSymbol=A%2FHRC%2F23%2F35&Language=E &DeviceType=Desktop&LangRequested=False

[98]https://undocs.org/Home/Mobile?FinalSymbol=E/C.12/1999/4&Language=E&DeviceType=Desktop&LangRequested=False

[99] https://uis.unesco.org/sites/default/files/documents/education-2030-incheon-framework-for-action-implementation-of-sdg4-2016-en_2.pdf

[100] http://hr-travaux.law.virginia.edu/document/iccpr/ecn4sr285/nid-2005

[101] http://uis.unesco.org/sites/default/files/documents/international-standard-classification-of-education-isced-2011-en.pdf

[102] In International Human Rights Law, the term 'freedom' is much more often used, but liberty is the term used in relation to education (Article 13 of the International Covenant on Economic, Social and Cultural Rights, as well as in Article 37 of the Convention on the Rights of the Child, related to children in conflict with the law).

[103] https://unesdoc.unesco.org/ark:/48223/pf0000109590

[104] https://www.ohchr.org/en/instruments-mechanisms/instruments/convention-rights-child

[105]https://tbinternet.ohchr.org/_layouts/15/treatybodyexternal/Download.aspx?symbolno=E%2FC.12%2F1999%2F4&Lang=es

[106]http://tbinternet.ohchr.org/_layouts/treatybodyexternal/Download.aspx?symbolno=E%2fC.12%2f1999%2f10&Lang=en

[107]https://tbinternet.ohchr.org/_layouts/15/treatybodyexternal/Download.aspx?symbolno=E%2F1991%2F23%28SUPP%29

[108] 0 https://undocs.org/Home/Mobile?FinalSymbol=E%2FCN.4%2F1999%-2F49&Language=E&DeviceType=Desktop&LangRequested=False

[109] https://www.ushistory.org/documents/economic_bill_of_rights.htm

[110] http://ap.ohchr.org/documents/alldocs.aspx?doc_id=1480

[111]https://undocs.org/Home/Mobile?FinalSymbol=CRC%2FGC%2F2001%2F1&Language=E&DeviceType=Desktop&LangRequested=False

[112] https://unesdoc.unesco.org/ark:/48223/pf0000231288

[113]https://undocs.org/Home/Mobile?FinalSymbol=E/C.12/1999/4&Language=E&DeviceType=Desktop&LangRequested=False

[114] https://unesdoc.unesco.org/ark:/48223/pf0000248254

[115] https://educacion.gob.ec/wp-content/uploads/downloads/2021/05/Ley-Organica-Reformatoria-a-la-Ley-Organica-de-Educacion-Intercultural-Registro-Oficial.pdf

[116] www.ilo.org/dyn/normlex/en/f?p=NORMLEXPUB:12100:0::NO::P12100_ILO_CODE:C138

[117] The appointment of Special Rapporteurs is, as above said, one of the "Special Procedures" or "Extra-conventional" mechanisms created by the former Commission on Human Rights to promote their respect. They are independent experts entrusted with a 'thematic mandate' (reporting and advising on a specific human right or an aspect of this right) or a 'geographic mandate' (reporting and advising on the human rights situation in a country, territory or region).

[118] At its origins was the Right to Education Project launched by the first Rapporteur on the Right to Education (Katarina Tomaševski), in 2000. After her premature death, it was relaunched in 2008 by five NGOs. Its multilingual electronic site is an exceptional source of information and documentation.

[119] https://www.india.gov.in/my-government/constitution-india

[120] http://indiankanoon.org/doc/1775396

[121]https://www.indiacode.nic.in/bitstream/123456789/2086/1/AAA35___2009.pdf

[122]https://undocs.org/Home/Mobile?FinalSymbol=E%2FC.12%2F1999%2F10&Language=E&DeviceType=Desktop&LangRequested=False

[123] *Jus Cogens* is a Latin term meaning literally 'Peremptory Law'. The denomination itself indicates that it does not express a new idea, but the concept entered International Law only with the Vienna Convention on the Law of Treaties (1969), whose Article 53 bears the title "Treaties conflicting with a peremptory norm of general international law ('jus cogens')".

[124]https://undocs.org/Home/Mobile?FinalSymbol=E%2FCN.4%2F2004%2F45&Language=E&DeviceType=Desktop&LangRequested=False

[125] https://myworld2015.files.wordpress.com/2014/12/wethepeoples-7million.pdf

[126] https://www.servat.unibe.ch/dfr/bv034269.html

Original text: *Das Wertsystem der Grundrechte findet seinen Mittelpunkt in der innerhalb der sozialen Gemeinschaft sich frei entfaltenden menschlichen Persönlichkeit und ihrer Würde (BVerfGE 6, 32 [41]; 7, 198 [205]).*

[127] http://indiankanoon.org/doc/40715

[128] http://www.saflii.org/za/cases/ZACC/1995/13.html

[129] http://www.hamoked.org/files/2013/113481_eng.pdf

[130] www.un.org/en/ga/search/view_doc.asp?symbol=A/C.3/SR.148

[131] Par. 122 in: http://uvallsc.s3.amazonaws.com/travaux/s3fs-public/E-2556__E-CN_4-669.pdf?iLfCJVZXmWKh2d_oZzyM_Uventu6NWy1

[132]https://undocs.org/Home/Mobile?FinalSymbol=E%2FCN.4%2F2001%2F52&Language=E&DeviceType=Desktop&LangRequested=False.

[133] http://ap.ohchr.org/documents/alldocs.aspx?doc_id=1920

[134] https://undocs.org/CRC/GC/2001/1

[135] https://www.ohchr.org/en/about-us/history/vienna-declaration

[136]https://undocs.org/Home/Mobile?FinalSymbol=E%2FC.12%2F1999%2F10&Language=E&DeviceType=Desktop&LangRequested=False

[137]https://uil.unesco.org/es/documento/uruguay-ley-general-educacion-ndeg-18437-promulgada-2008#:~:text=Uruguay%3A%20Ley%20%20General%20de%20Educaci%C3%B3n,N%C2%B0%2018437%2C%20%20promulgada%20en%202008

[138] https://www.gesetze-im-internet.de/gg/index.html

[139] The German Federal Constitutional Court said (*1 BvR 1181/10*, para. 109):

> The free State under the Basic Law is characterised by openness to the diversity of religious and ideological convictions and bases that openness upon a concept of humanity characterised by human dignity and the free development of one's personality in self-determination under one's own responsibility (cf. BVerfGE 41, 29; 108, 282).

(https://www.bundesverfassungsgericht.de/SharedDocs/Entscheidungen/EN/2015/01/rs20150127_1bvr047110en.html)

[140] *Ordre Public*: set of values and principles of life of a legally-politically organised community. They are "principles which, for reasons of the common good, are also to be binding for the shaping of legal relations between individuals and are therefore withdrawn from the dominion of the private will", as said the German Federal Constitutional Court (1 BvR 400/51, 15 January 1958, para. 27): https://www.bundesverfassungsgericht.de/SharedDocs/Downloads/DE/1958/01/rs19580115_1bvr040051.pdf?__blob=publicationFile&v=1)

[141] https://undocs.org/CRC/GC/2001/1

[142] https://www.unesco.org/en/legal-affairs/constitution

[143] https://undocs.org/Home/Mobile?FinalSymbol=A%2FRES%2F217(III)&Language=E&DeviceType=Desktop&LangRequested=False

[144] https://unric.org/en/human-rights-75/

[145] See, for example: https://epale.ec.europa.eu/en/content/reinforcing-european-dimension-education-commission-launches-future-learning-package

[146] https://unesdoc.unesco.org/ark:/48223/pf0000243899

[147] https://www.ohchr.org/en/instruments-mechanisms/instruments/convention-rights-child

[148] https://www.ohchr.org/EN/Issues/Education/Training/Pages/UNDHREducationTraining.aspx

[149] https://unesdoc.unesco.org/ark:/48223/pf0000089326

[150] https://www.ohchr.org/en/instruments-mechanisms/instruments/universal-declaration-human-genome-and-human-rights

[151] http://ap.ohchr.org/documents/alldocs.aspx?doc_id=9100

[152] For instance, according to the Social Charter of the Americas (OAS, 2012): "Member States commit to ensuring equal and universal access to quality primary and secondary education and promote access to education at all levels, with an inclusive approach, especially early childhood education, in accordance with their domestic law." (Article 19)
(https://view.officeapps.live.com/op/view.aspx?src=https%3A%2F%2Fwww.oas.org%2Fdocs%2Fpublications%2Fsocial_charter_of_the_americas.doc&wdOrigin=BROWSELINK)

[153] https://www.unesco.org/en/legal-affairs/constitution

[154] In this respect, the African Youth Charter (2006) deserves to be quoted. After stating "Every young person shall have the right to education of good quality" (Article 13.1), it provides:

> 4. States Parties shall take all appropriate measures with a view to achieving full realisation of this right and shall, in particular:
>
> ...
>
> n) Promote culturally appropriate, age specific sexuality, and responsible parenthood education;

(https://au.int/en/treaties/african-youth-charter)

[155] www.corteconstitucional.gov.co/relatoria/1995/T-337-95.htm

[156] https://unesdoc.unesco.org/ark:/48223/pf0000245656

[157] In this connection, the German Federal Constitutional Court made some interesting considerations in a Case concerned with disabled children (*1 BvR 9/97*, 8 October 1997, para. 53-55):

> By means of the rule concerning State supervision of schools which is set down in Art.7 Sec.1 GC, the State has the authority to plan and organise the school system with the aim of providing a system that gives young people the educational possibilities according to their individual abilities and today's social needs. For this reason, the organisational structure of schools, the structural arrangement of the education system and the setting of the training and teaching objectives are subjects of the State (see BVerfGE 34, 165; 45, 400; 53, 185). […]
> Also, for their upbringing and education in the area of schools the State has at least a *de facto* monopoly, the disabled as well as the non-disabled have the duty to attend a public school. Taking this into consideration following Art. 2 Sec. 1, Art. 6 Sec. 2 Phrase 1 in connection with Art. 3 Sec. 3 Phrase 2 GC, the State has the duty to principally provide schools for disabled children and juveniles that guarantee a proper school upbringing and education. The kind and intensity of the disability as well as the provisions of the school and the level of the class have to be taken into consideration under the premises of the state of the art of pedagogic and scientific knowledge.

(https://www.bundesverfassungsgericht.de/SharedDocs/Downloads/EN/1997/10/rs19971008_1bvr000997en.pdf?__blob=publicationFile&v=3)

[158]https://tbinternet.ohchr.org/_layouts/15/treatybodyexternal/Download.aspx?symbolno=CRC/C/GC/25&Lang=en

[159] https://www.europarl.europa.eu/thinktank/en/document/EPRS_STU(2021)696170

[160] https://education.ec.europa.eu/sites/default/files/document-library-docs/deap-swd-sept2020_en.pdf

[161] https://www.un.org/en/about-us/universal-declaration-of-human-rights

[162] https://www.vatican.va/archive/ENG0839/_INDEX.HTM

[163] The Committee on Economic, Social and Cultural Rights said in its General Comment 13 (E/C.12/1999/10), note 18: "The Committee notes that, although it is absent from Article 26.2 of the Declaration, the drafters [of the respective International Covenant] expressly included the dignity of the human personality as one of the mandatory objectives to which all education is to be directed (Article 13.1)."
https://undocs.org/Home/Mobile?FinalSymbol=E%2FC.12%2F1999%2F10&Language=E&DeviceType=Desktop&LangRequested=False

[164] Academic studies reveal that many serial killers had childhoods with a lot of violence and abuse, sometimes leading to the murder of their own father and/or mother.

[165] https://www.ohchr.org/en/professionalinterest/pages/crc.aspx

[166]https://tbinternet.ohchr.org/_layouts/15/treatybodyexternal/Download.aspx?symbolno=E%2FC.12%2F1999%2F4&Lang=es

[167] The South African Constitutional Court said in *August and Another v Electoral Commission and Others* (Case CCT 8/99, 1 April 1999): "The vote of each and every citizen is a badge of dignity and of personhood. Quite literally, it says that everybody counts."

(para. 17)
(http://www.saflii.org/za/cases/ZACC/1999/3.html)
[168] The African Youth Charter (2006) commands: "Provide free and compulsory basic education and take steps to minimise the indirect costs of education" (Article 13.4.a). (https://au.int/en/treaties/african-youth-charter)
[169] https://internationalcommunities.org/wp-content/uploads/2017/07/principles-on-implemention-of-esc-rights-in-african-charter.pdf
[170] An approach that, in the US, divides liberal and conservative tendencies when it comes to the interpretation of the Federal Constitution.
[171] https://treaties.un.org/doc/Publication/UNTS/Volume%201155/v1155.pdf
[172]https://www.undocs.org/Home/Mobile?FinalSymbol=CRPD%2FC%2FGC%2F4&Language=E&DeviceType=Desktop&LangRequested=False
[173] The German Federal Constitutional Court said (*BVerfGE) 121, 69*, para. 71):

> The child has its own dignity and rights. [...] This also applies to the relationship between parents and their child. The parental right vis-à-vis the child is justified by the fact that the child requires protection and help so that it can develop into a responsible member of society [...]. This right is therefore inextricably linked to the parents' duty to provide the child with this protection and assistance for its welfare.

(https://www.servat.unibe.ch/dfr/bv121069.html)

[174] http://assembly.coe.int/nw/xml/XRef/Xref-XML2HTML-en.asp?fileid=25353
[175] The German Federal Constitutional Court remarked (*1 BvR 471/10*, 27 January 2015, para. 109): "The Basic Law lays down for the State as the home of all citizens [...] the duty of religious and ideological neutrality."
(https://www.bundesverfassungsgericht.de/SharedDocs/Entscheidungen/DE/2015/01/rs20150127_1bvr047110.html)
[176]https://static1.squarespace.com/static/5c2d081daf2096648cc801da/t/5c933a1be79c70cf6cc27edd/1553152561554/Abidjan-Principles-EN.pdf
[177] https://static1.squarespace.com/static/5c2d081daf2096648cc801da/t/61484ef2125d785da37eb98d/1632128758265/ABIDJAN+PRINCIPLES_+ENGLISH_August2021.pdf
[178] https://es.wikiquote.org/wiki/Mario_Benedetti
[179] *Dear father!*
I am saying goodbye to you before I die. We would so love to live, but they won't let us, and we will die. I am so scared of this death, because the small children are thrown alive into the [burning] pit. Goodbye forever. I kiss you tenderly.
Yours J.

Judith Wishnyatskaya, 12 years old, 31 July 1942
Message thrown from the train that carried her and her mother to a Nazi extermination camp. Words reproduced on the floor of the Room of Dimensions of the Memorial to the Jews of Europe murdered by Nazism, in Berlin.

[180]https://www.youthpolicy.org/library/wp-content/uploads/library/1999_UNICEF_State_of_the_worlds_Children_Report_Eng.pdf

[181] P. 188 in:
https://unesdoc.unesco.org/ark:/48223/pf0000102734/PDF/102734engo.pdf.multi
[182]https://ia800302.us.archive.org/17/items/TheProphetByKhalilGibran/The_Prophet_by_Khalil_Gibran.pdf
[183] https://unesdoc.unesco.org/ark:/48223/pf0000245656
[184] Gordian Knot is an expression, originating in a Greek legend, which means a problem very difficult or impossible to solve.
[185] http://www.un-documents.net/gdrc1924.htm

www.ingramcontent.com/pod-product-compliance
Lightning Source LLC
LaVergne TN
LVHW101504200926
848483LV00001B/225
* 9 7 8 1 8 0 4 4 1 5 1 2 2 *